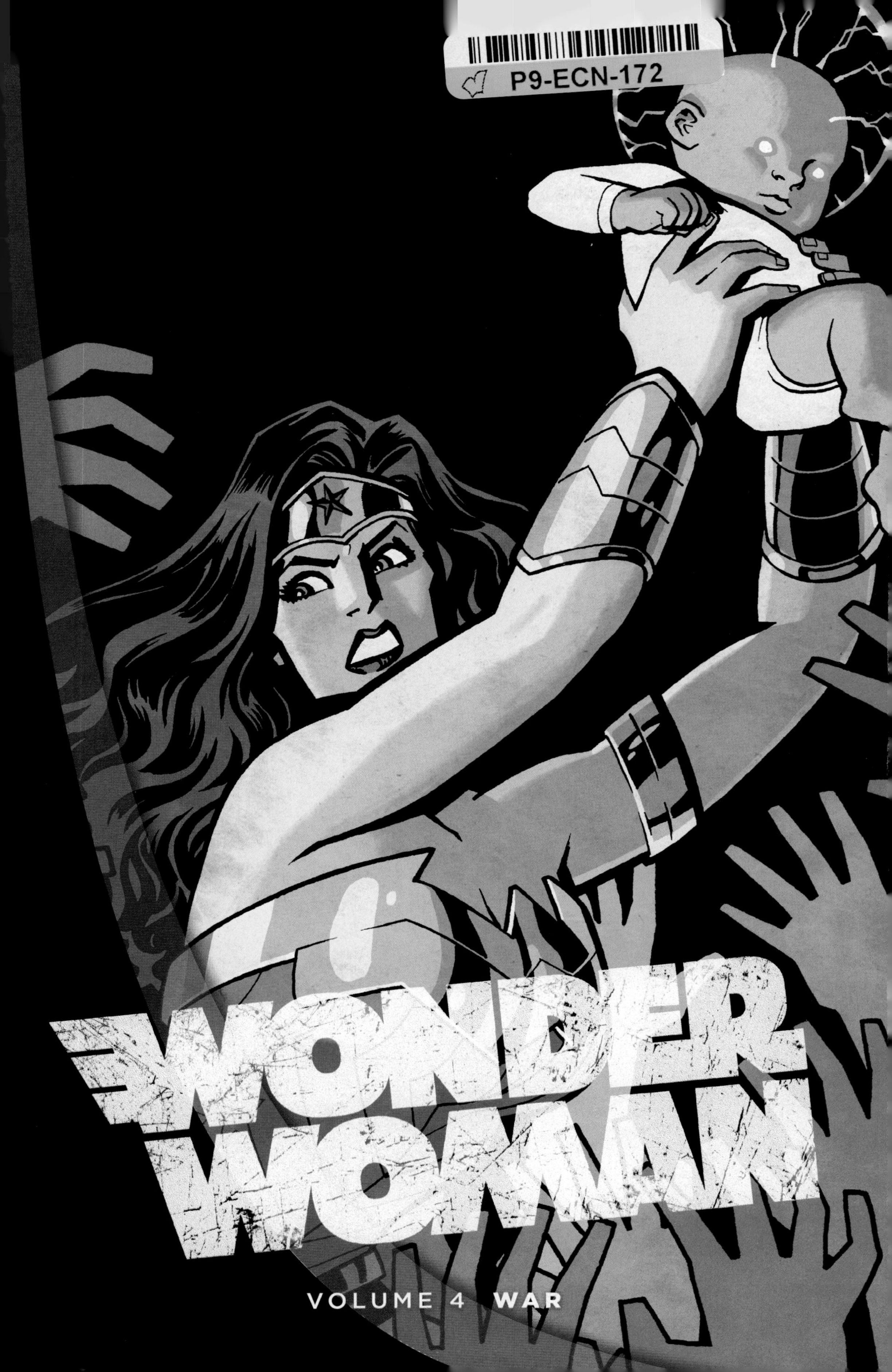
WONDER WOMAN
VOLUME 4 WAR

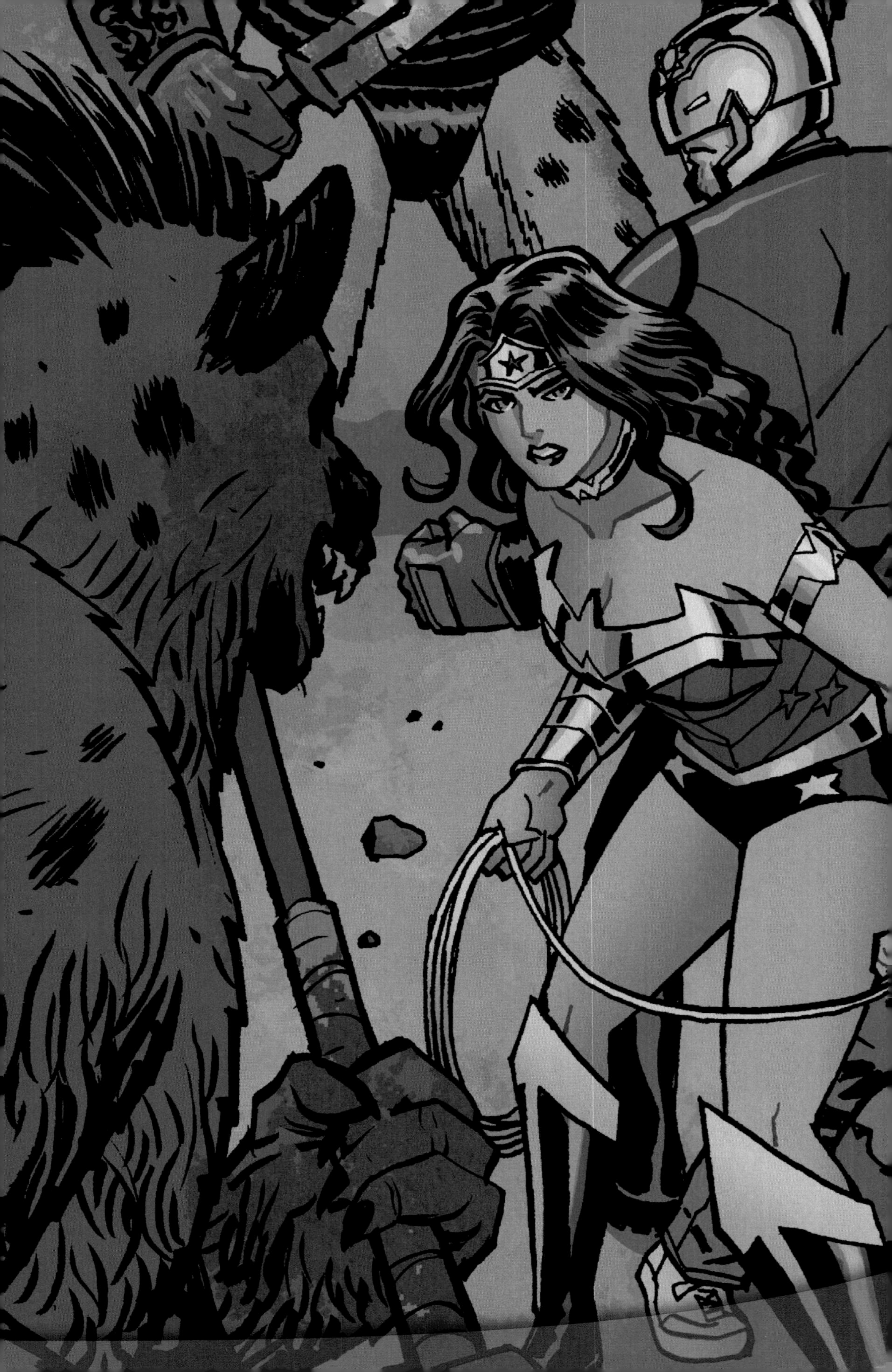

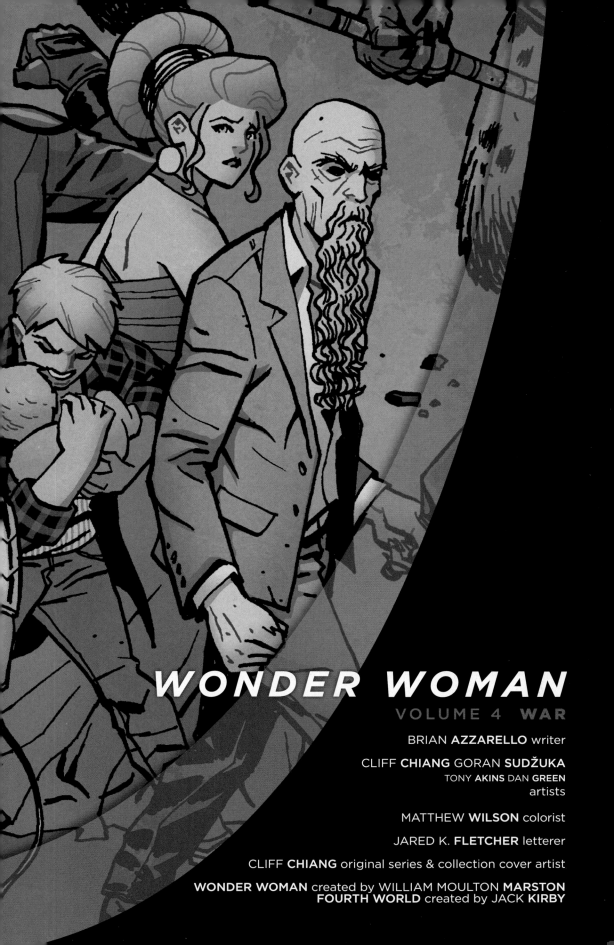

WONDER WOMAN

VOLUME 4 WAR

BRIAN **AZZARELLO** writer

CLIFF **CHIANG** GORAN **SUDŽUKA**

TONY **AKINS** DAN **GREEN**
artists

MATTHEW **WILSON** colorist

JARED K. **FLETCHER** letterer

CLIFF **CHIANG** original series & collection cover artist

WONDER WOMAN created by WILLIAM MOULTON **MARSTON**
FOURTH WORLD created by JACK **KIRBY**

MATT IDELSON Editor – Original Series CHRIS CONROY Associate Editor – Original Series
RACHEL PINNELAS Editor ROBBIN BROSTERMAN Design Director – Books
ROBBIE BIEDERMAN Publication Design

BOB HARRAS Senior VP – Editor-in-Chief, DC Comics

DIANE NELSON President DAN DIDIO and JIM LEE Co-Publishers GEOFF JOHNS Chief Creative Officer
AMIT DESAI Senior VP – Marketing and Franchise Management
AMY GENKINS Senior VP – Business and Legal Affairs NAIRI GARDINER Senior VP – Finance
JEFF BOISON VP – Publishing Planning MARK CHIARELLO VP – Art Direction and Design
JOHN CUNNINGHAM VP – Marketing TERRI CUNNINGHAM VP – Editorial Administration
LARRY GANEM VP – Talent Relations and Services ALISON GILL Senior VP – Manufacturing and Operations
HANK KANALZ Senior VP – Vertigo and Integrated Publishing JAY KOGAN VP – Business and Legal Affairs, Publishing
JACK MAHAN VP – Business Affairs, Talent NICK NAPOLITANO VP – Manufacturing Administration SUE POHJA VP – Book Sales
FRED RUIZ VP – Manufacturing Operations COURTNEY SIMMONS Senior VP – Publicity BOB WAYNE Senior VP – Sales

WONDER WOMAN VOLUME 4: WAR

DC Comics, 1700 Broadway, New York, NY 10019
A Warner Bros. Entertainment Company.
Printed by R. R. Donnelly,, Salem, VA, USA. 8/29/14. First Printing.
ISBN: 978-1-4012-4954-0

SUSTAINABLE
FORESTRY
INITIATIVE

Certified Chain of Custody
20% Certified Forest Content,
80% Certified Sourcing
www.sfiprogram.org
SFI-01042
APPLIES TO TEXT STOCK ONLY

Library of Congress Cataloging-in-Publication Data

Azzarello, Brian, author.
Wonder Woman. Volume 4, War / Brian Azzarello; [illustrated by] Cliff Chiang, Tony Akins.
pages cm. — (The New 52!)
ISBN 978-1-4012-4954-0
1. Graphic novels. I. Chiang, Cliff, illustrator. II. Akins, Tony, illustrator. III. Title. IV. Title: War.
PN6728.W6A994 2014
741.5'973—dc23
2013046159

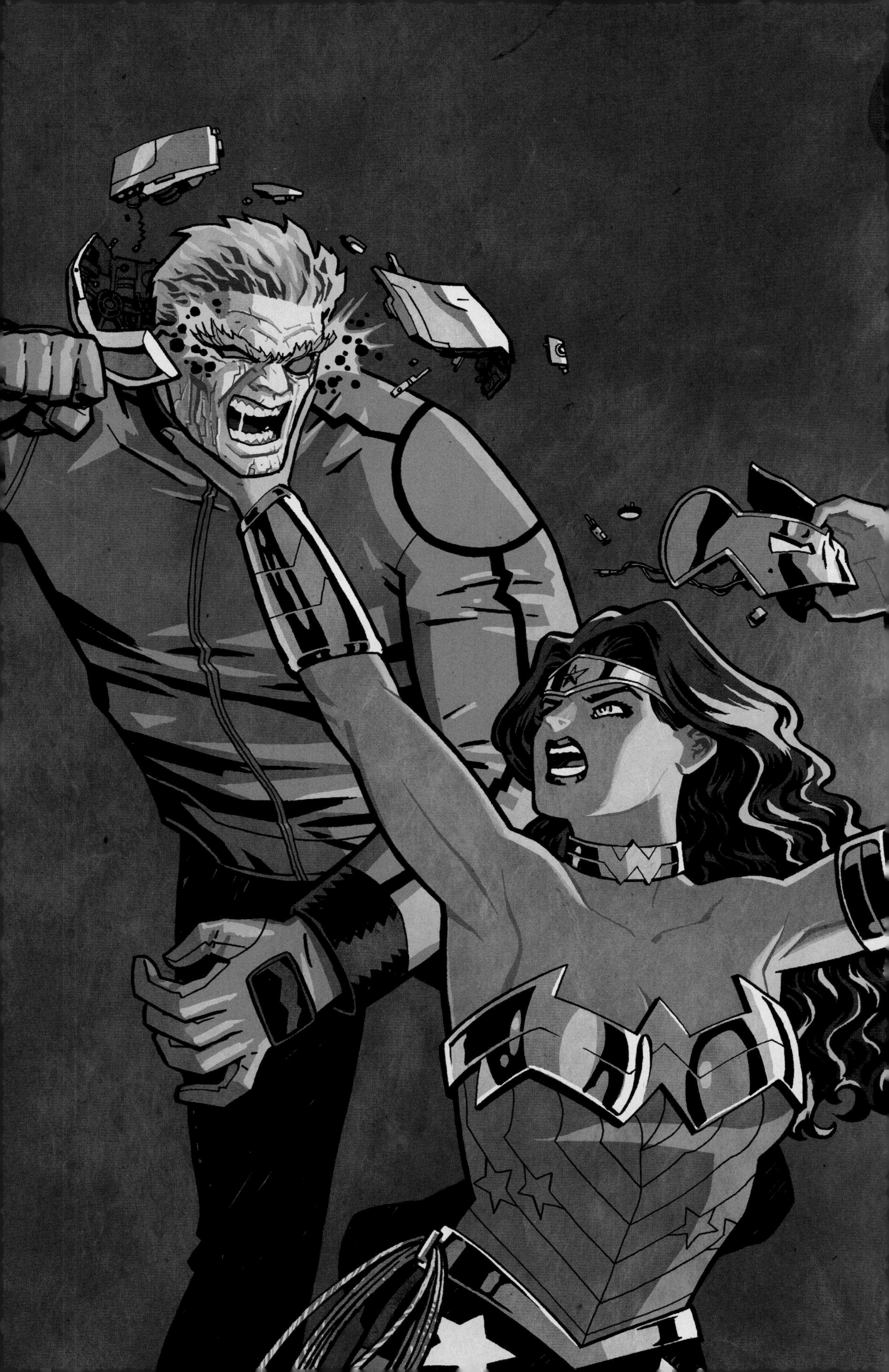

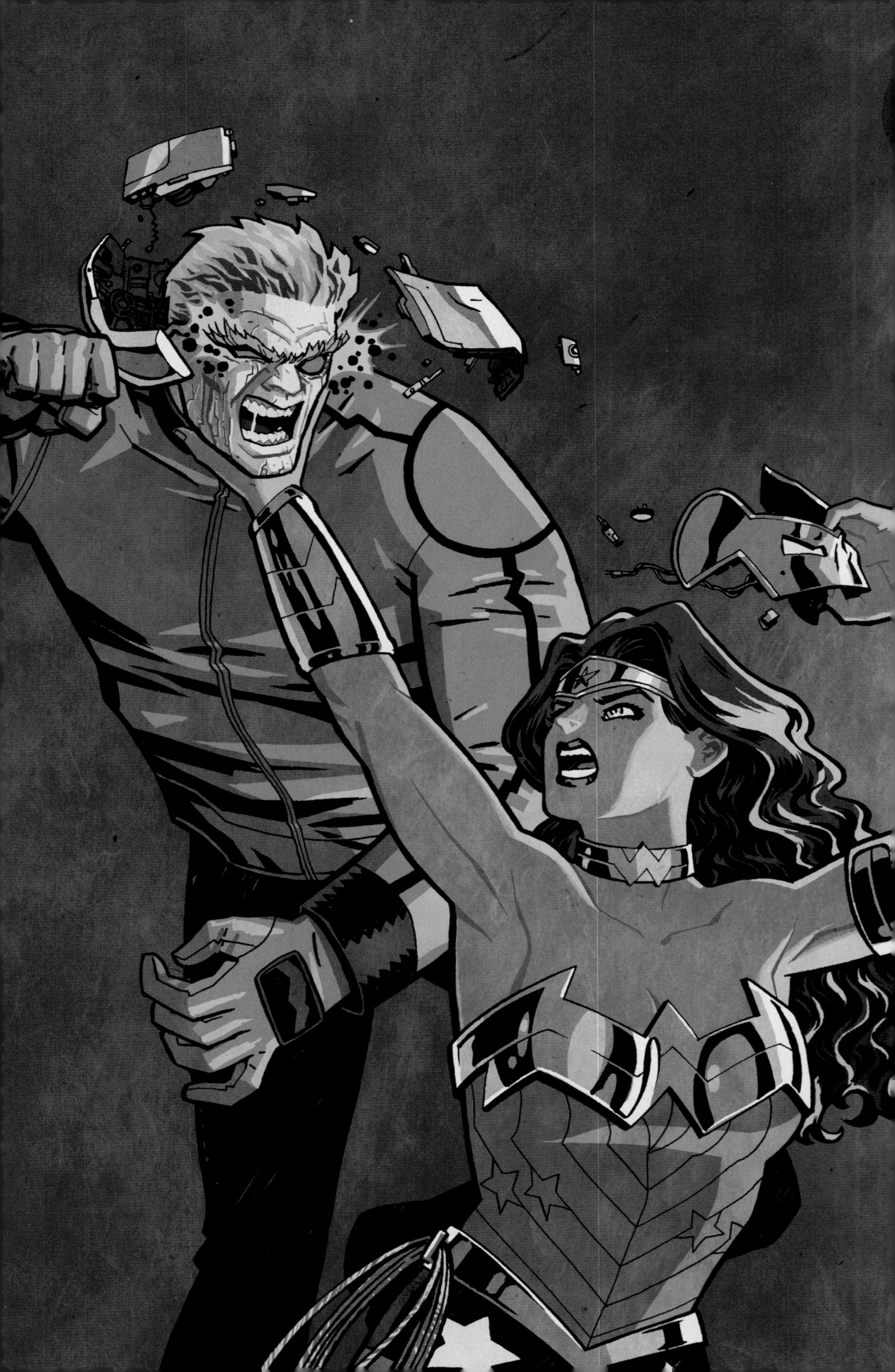

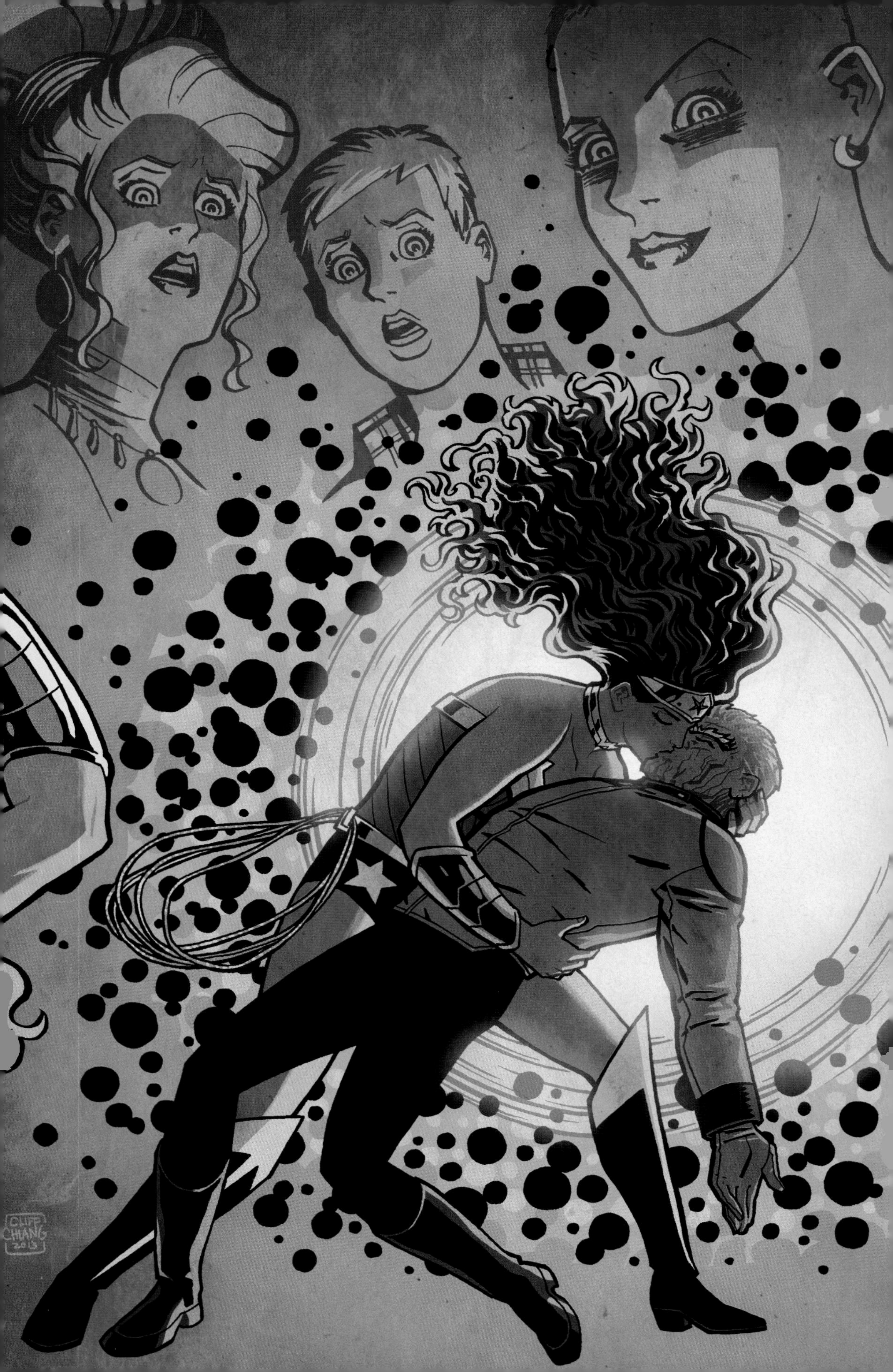
CLIFF
CHIANG
2013

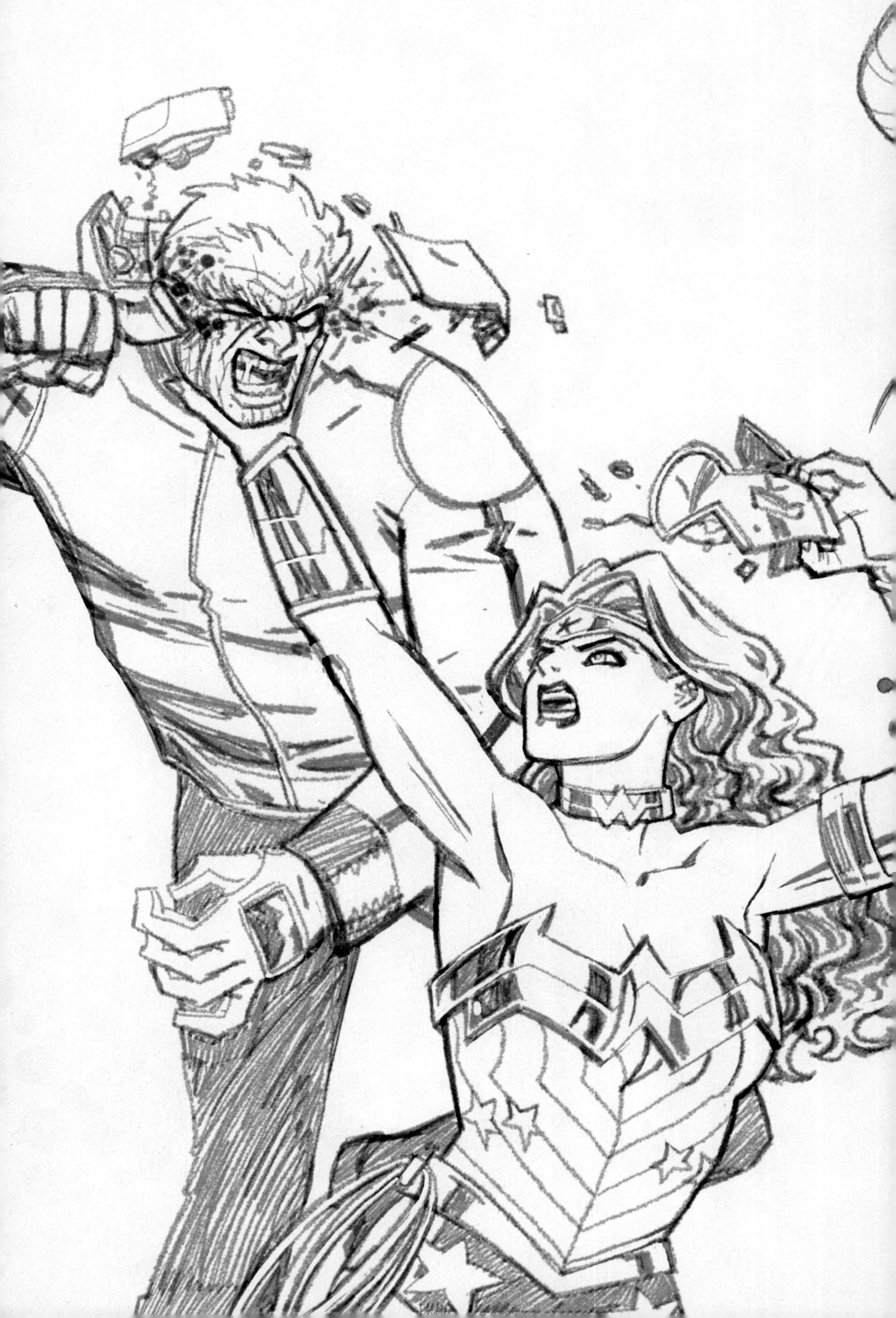

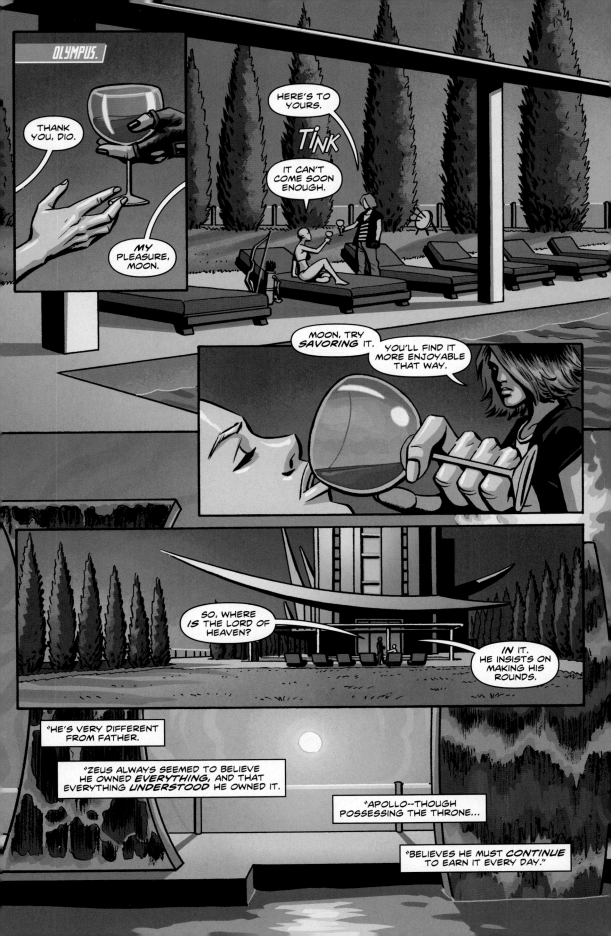

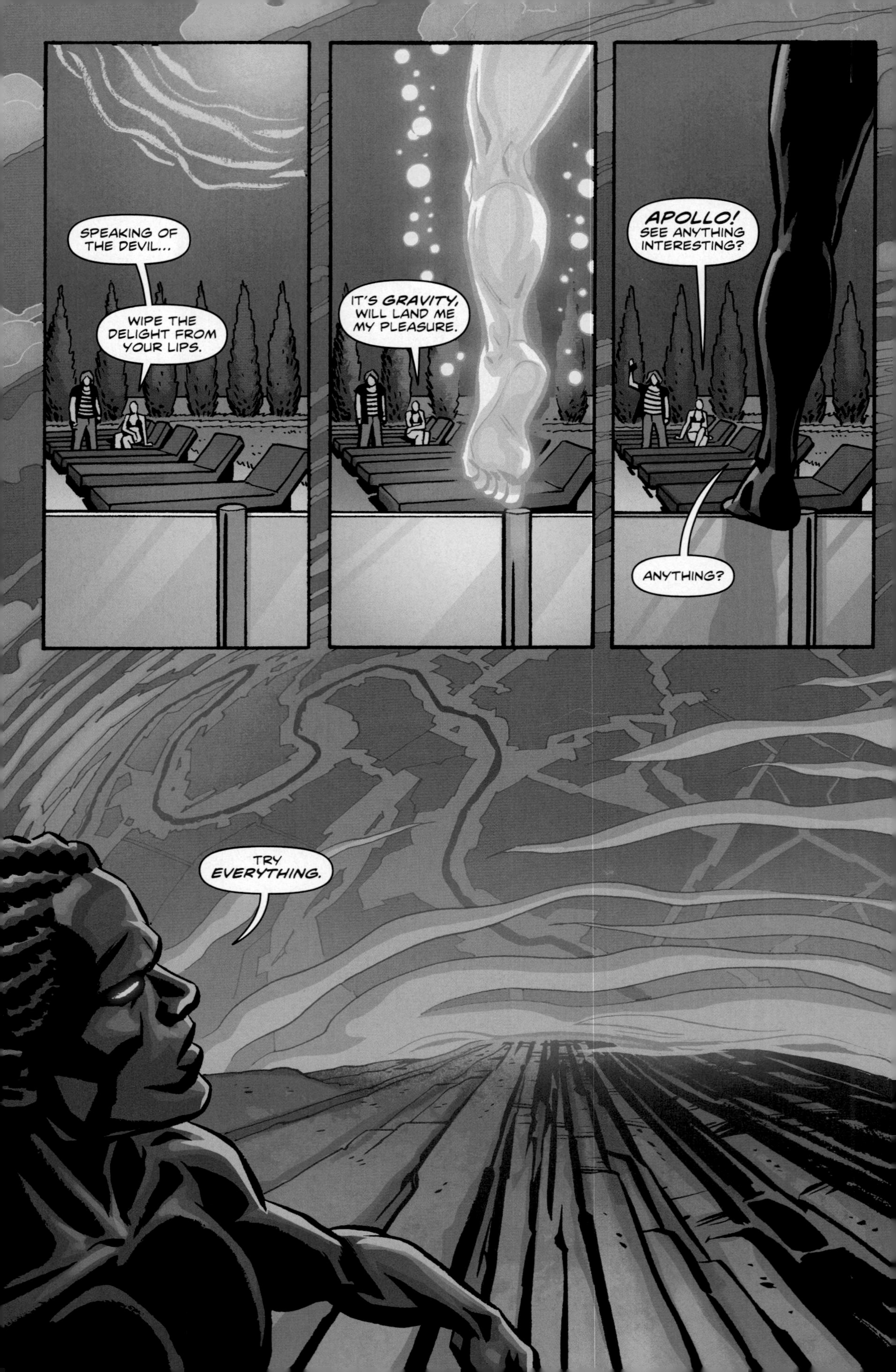
SPEAKING OF THE DEVIL...
WIPE THE DELIGHT FROM YOUR LIPS.
IT'S *GRAVITY,* WILL LAND ME MY PLEASURE.
APOLLO! SEE ANYTHING INTERESTING?
ANYTHING?
TRY *EVERYTHING.*

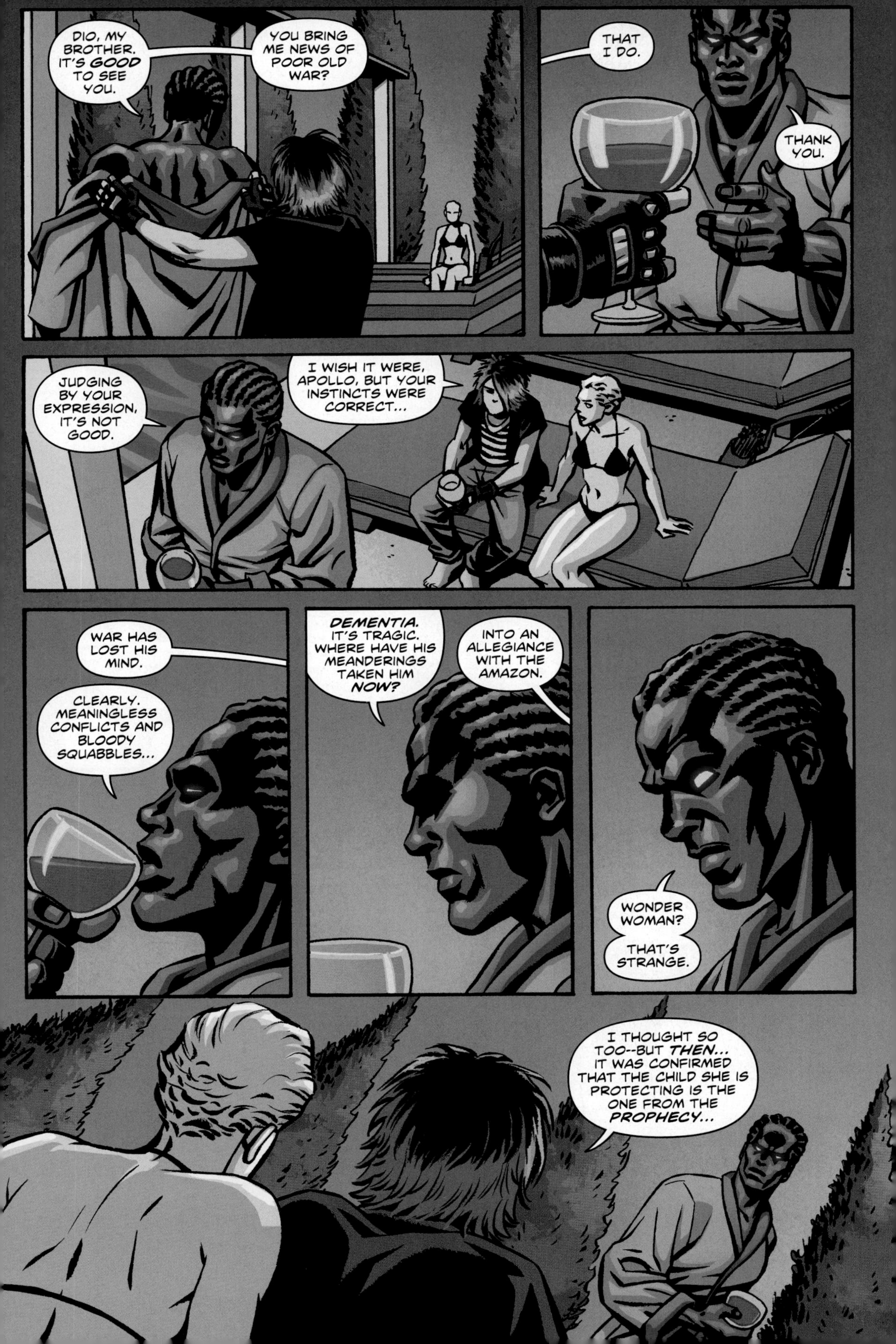
DIO, MY BROTHER. IT'S *GOOD* TO SEE YOU.
YOU BRING ME NEWS OF POOR OLD WAR?
THAT I DO.
THANK YOU.
JUDGING BY YOUR EXPRESSION, IT'S NOT GOOD.
I WISH IT WERE, APOLLO, BUT YOUR INSTINCTS WERE CORRECT...
WAR HAS LOST HIS MIND.
CLEARLY. MEANINGLESS CONFLICTS AND BLOODY SQUABBLES...
DEMENTIA. IT'S TRAGIC. WHERE HAVE HIS MEANDERINGS TAKEN HIM *NOW?*
INTO AN ALLEGIANCE WITH THE AMAZON.
WONDER WOMAN?
THAT'S STRANGE.
I THOUGHT SO TOO--BUT *THEN...* IT WAS CONFIRMED THAT THE CHILD SHE IS PROTECTING IS THE ONE FROM THE *PROPHECY...*

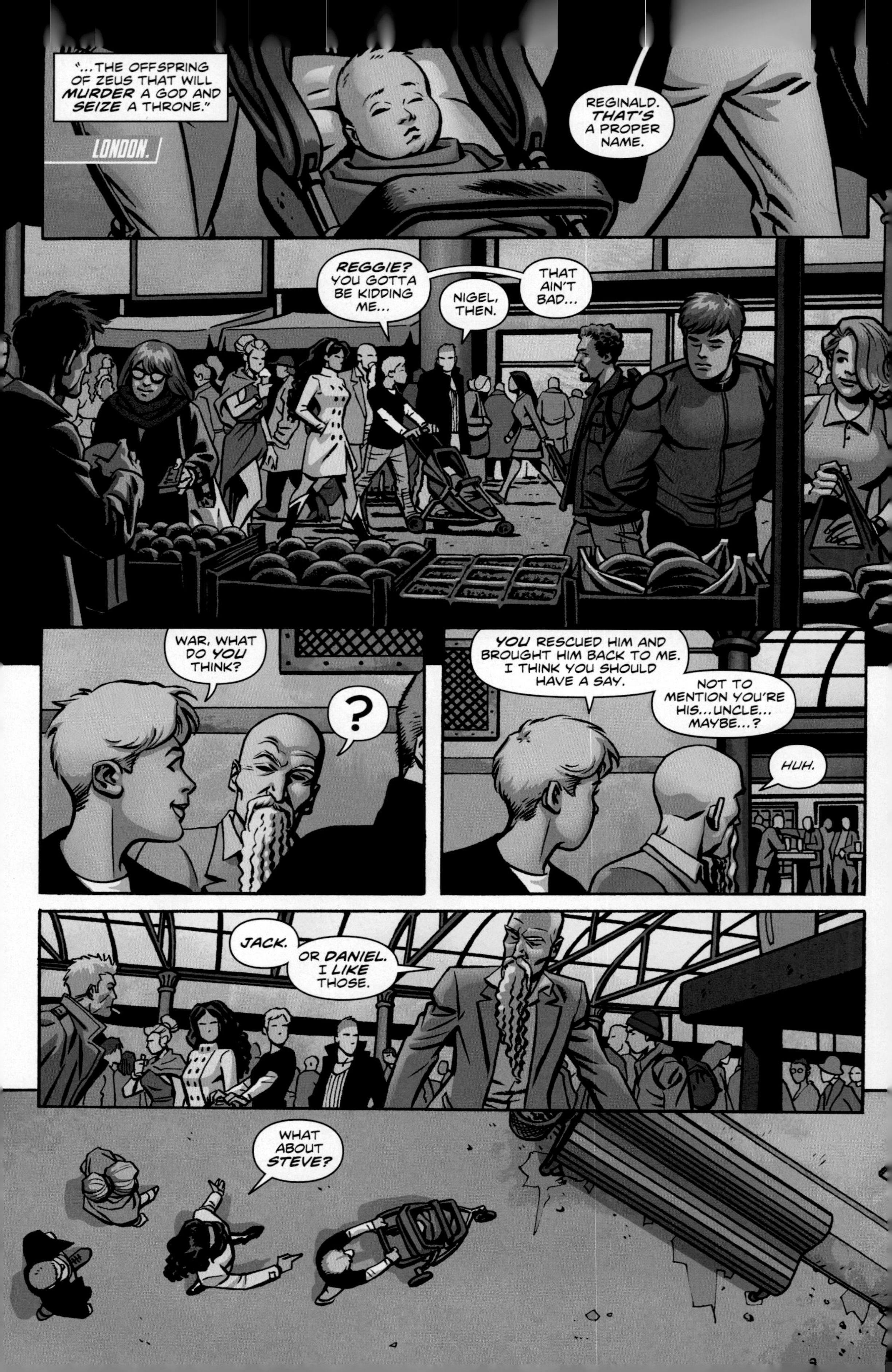
"...THE OFFSPRING OF ZEUS THAT WILL MURDER A GOD AND SEIZE A THRONE."
LONDON.
REGINALD. THAT'S A PROPER NAME.
REGGIE? YOU GOTTA BE KIDDING ME...
NIGEL, THEN.
THAT AIN'T BAD...
WAR, WHAT DO YOU THINK?
?
YOU RESCUED HIM AND BROUGHT HIM BACK TO ME. I THINK YOU SHOULD HAVE A SAY.
NOT TO MENTION YOU'RE HIS...UNCLE... MAYBE...?
HUH.
JACK.
OR DANIEL. I LIKE THOSE.
WHAT ABOUT STEVE?

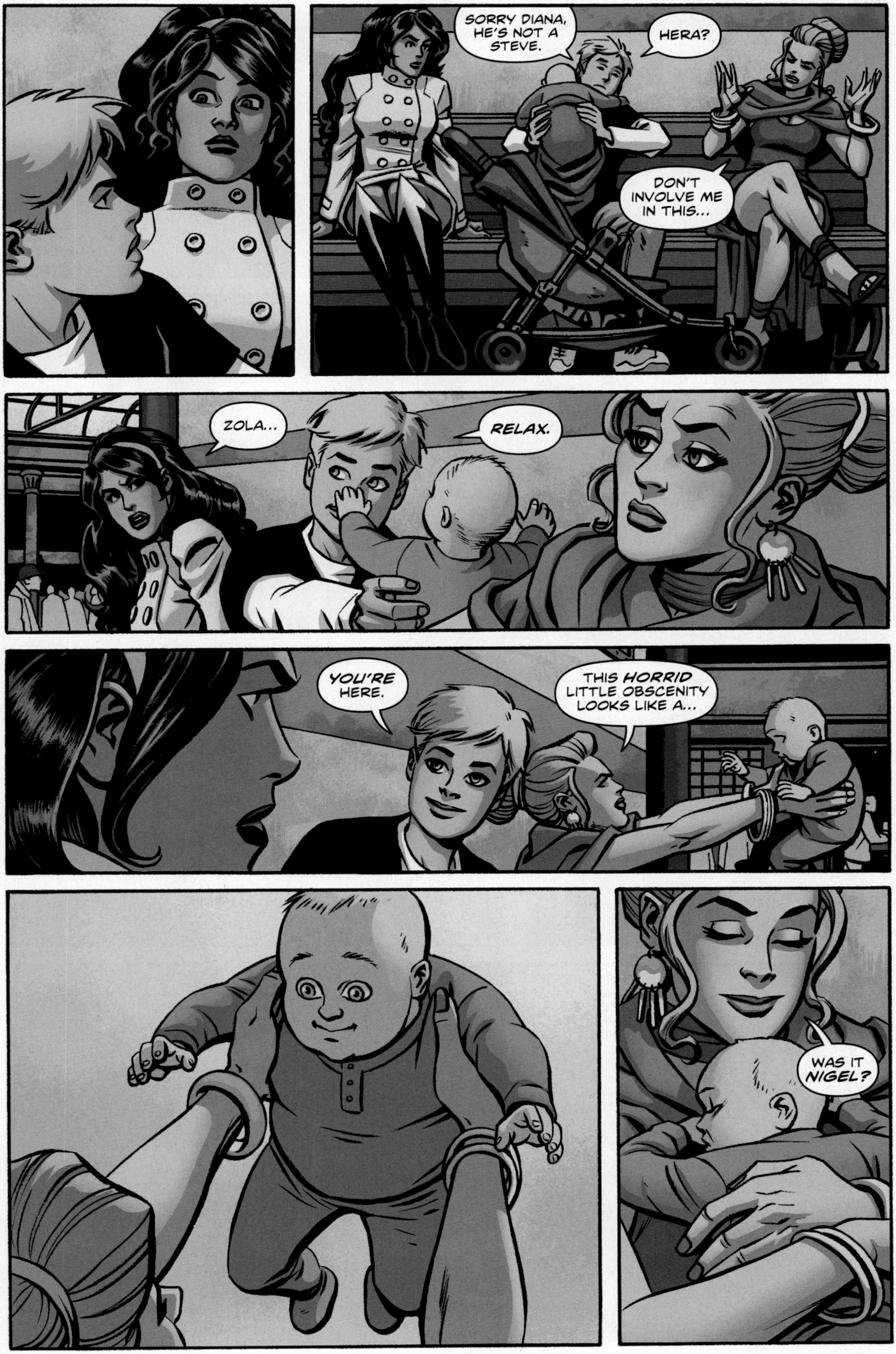
SORRY DIANA, HE'S NOT A STEVE.
HERA?
DON'T INVOLVE ME IN THIS...
ZOLA...
RELAX.
YOU'RE HERE.
THIS HORRID LITTLE OBSCENITY LOOKS LIKE A...
WAS IT NIGEL?

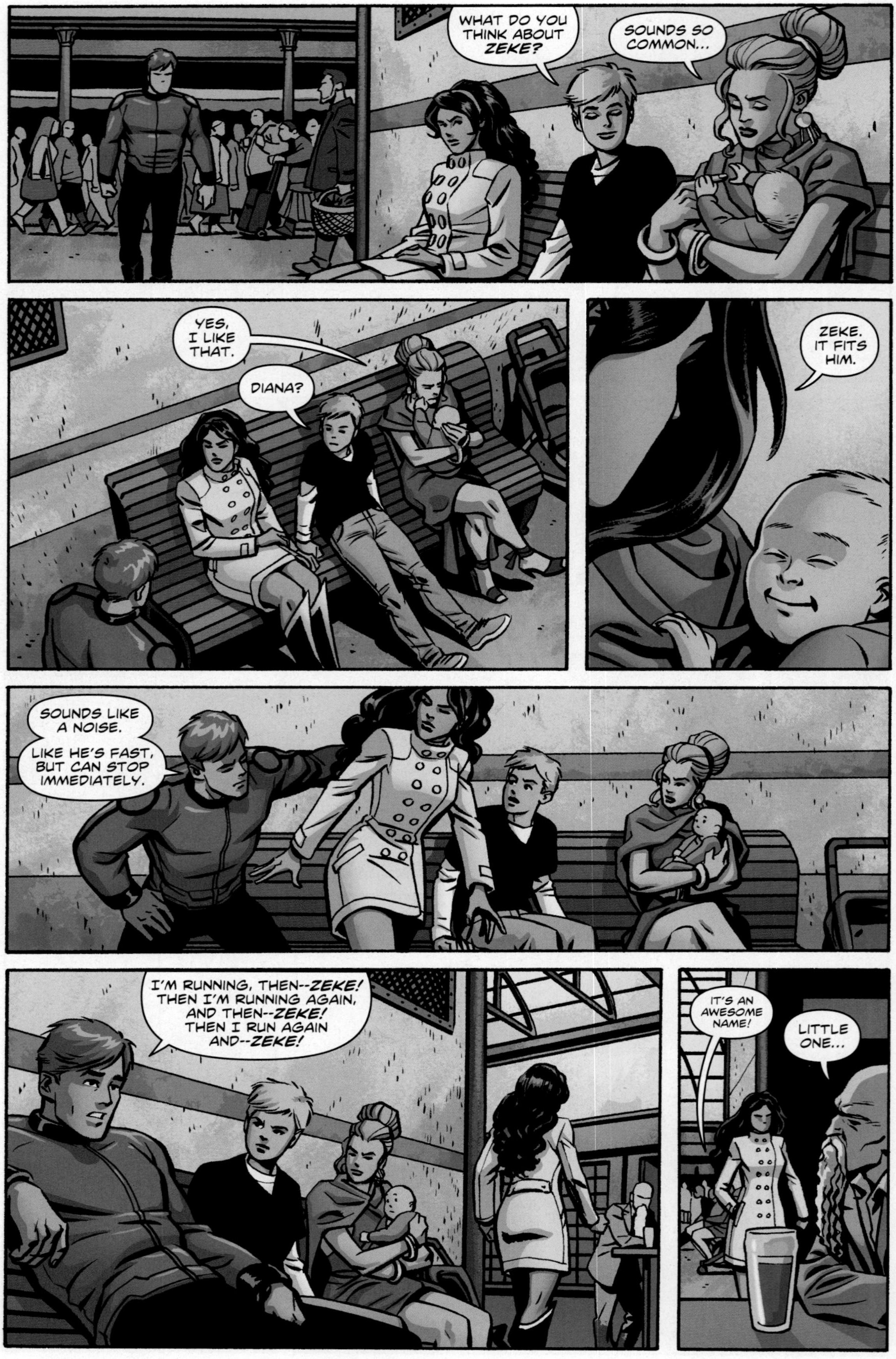
WHAT DO YOU THINK ABOUT ZEKE?
SOUNDS SO COMMON...
YES, I LIKE THAT.
DIANA?
ZEKE. IT FITS HIM.
SOUNDS LIKE A NOISE.
LIKE HE'S FAST, BUT CAN STOP IMMEDIATELY.
I'M RUNNING, THEN--ZEKE! THEN I'M RUNNING AGAIN, AND THEN--ZEKE! THEN I RUN AGAIN AND--ZEKE!
IT'S AN AWESOME NAME!
LITTLE ONE...

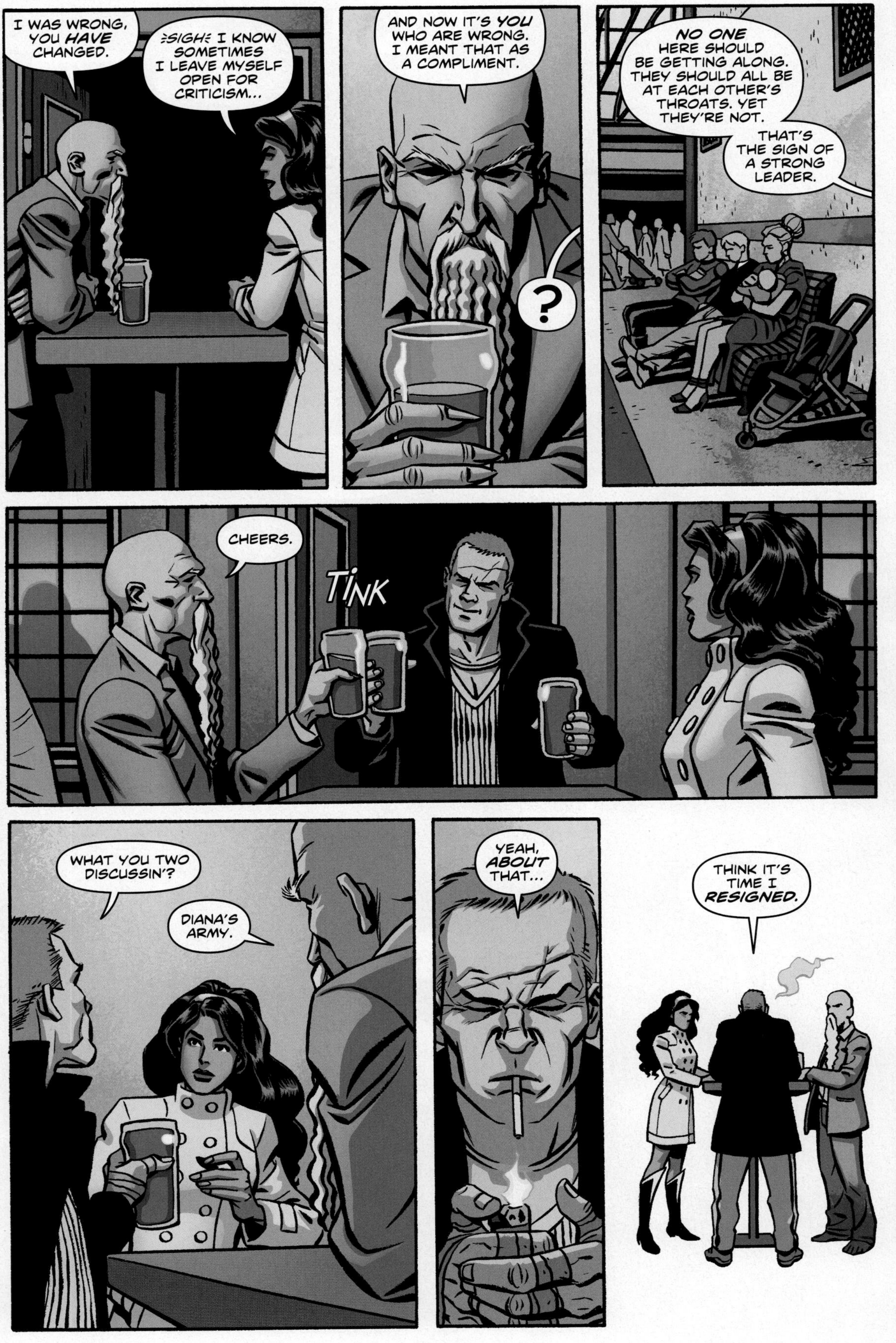

I WAS WRONG, YOU HAVE CHANGED.
=SIGH= I KNOW SOMETIMES I LEAVE MYSELF OPEN FOR CRITICISM...
AND NOW IT'S YOU WHO ARE WRONG. I MEANT THAT AS A COMPLIMENT.
?
NO ONE HERE SHOULD BE GETTING ALONG. THEY SHOULD ALL BE AT EACH OTHER'S THROATS. YET THEY'RE NOT.
THAT'S THE SIGN OF A STRONG LEADER.
CHEERS.
TINK
WHAT YOU TWO DISCUSSIN'?
DIANA'S ARMY.
YEAH, ABOUT THAT...
THINK IT'S TIME I RESIGNED.

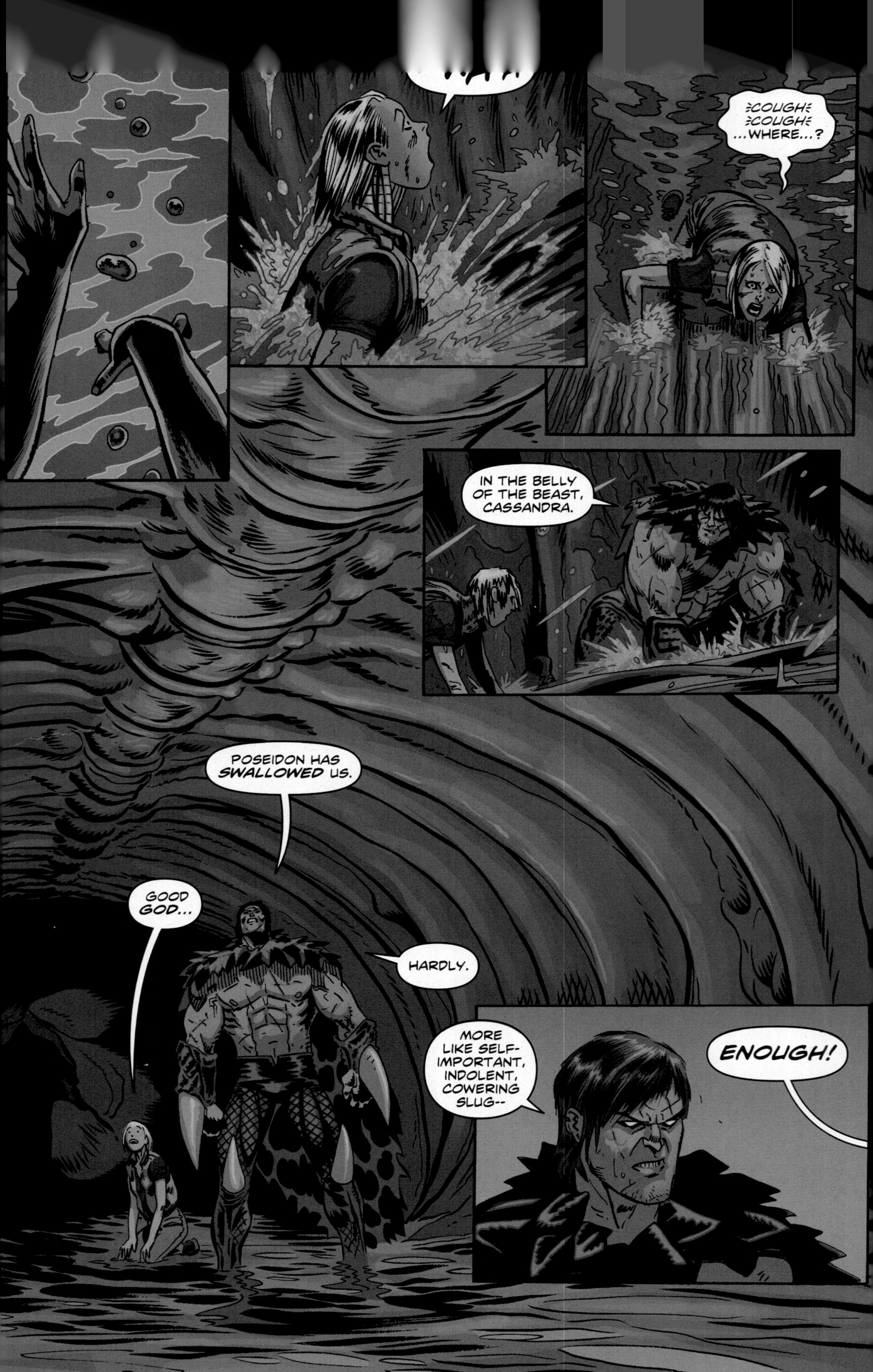
COUGH COUGH ...WHERE...?
IN THE BELLY OF THE BEAST, CASSANDRA.
POSEIDON HAS SWALLOWED US.
GOOD GOD...
HARDLY.
MORE LIKE SELF-IMPORTANT, INDOLENT, COWERING SLUG--
ENOUGH!

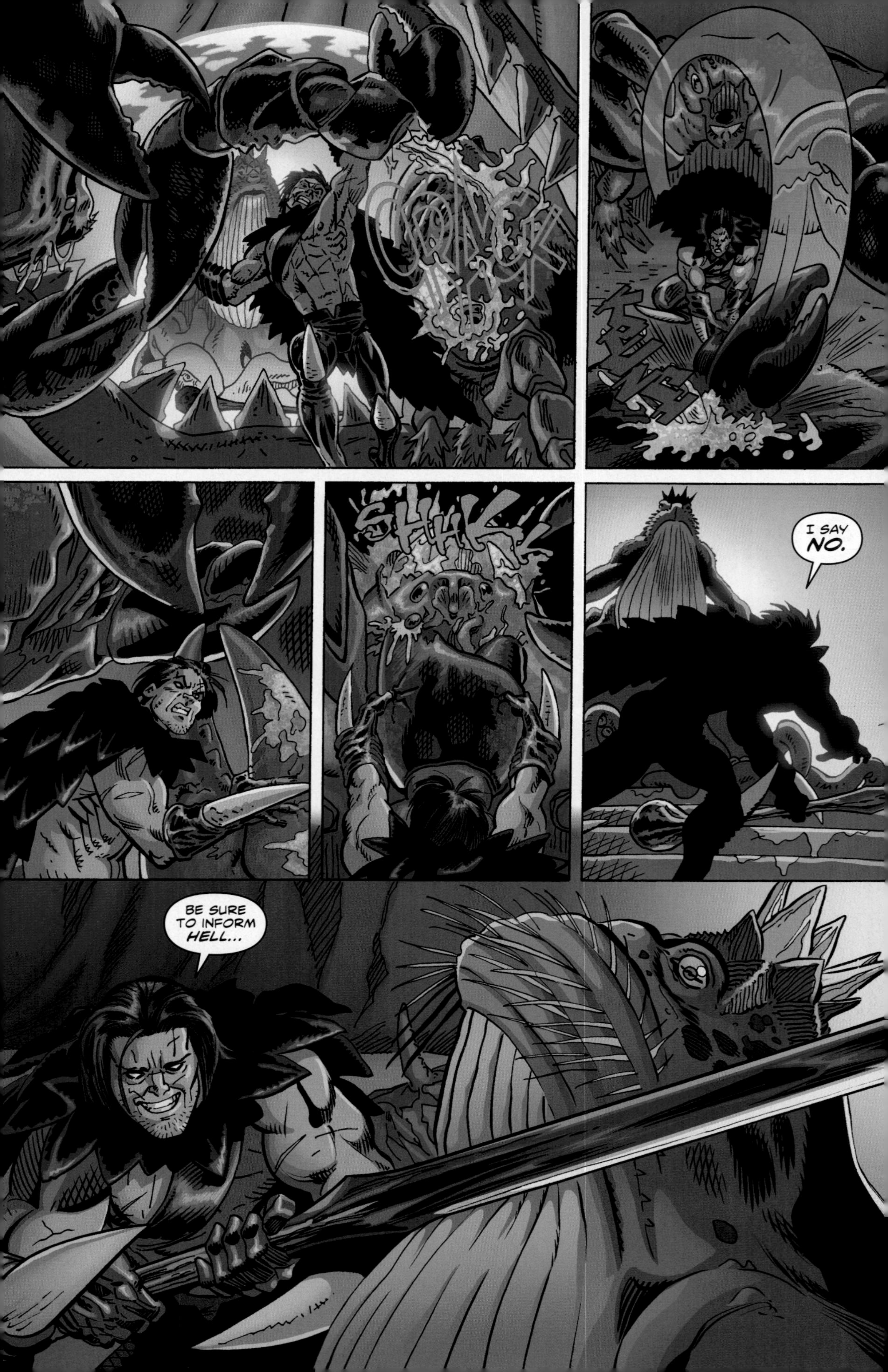
I SAY *NO.*
BE SURE TO INFORM *HELL...*

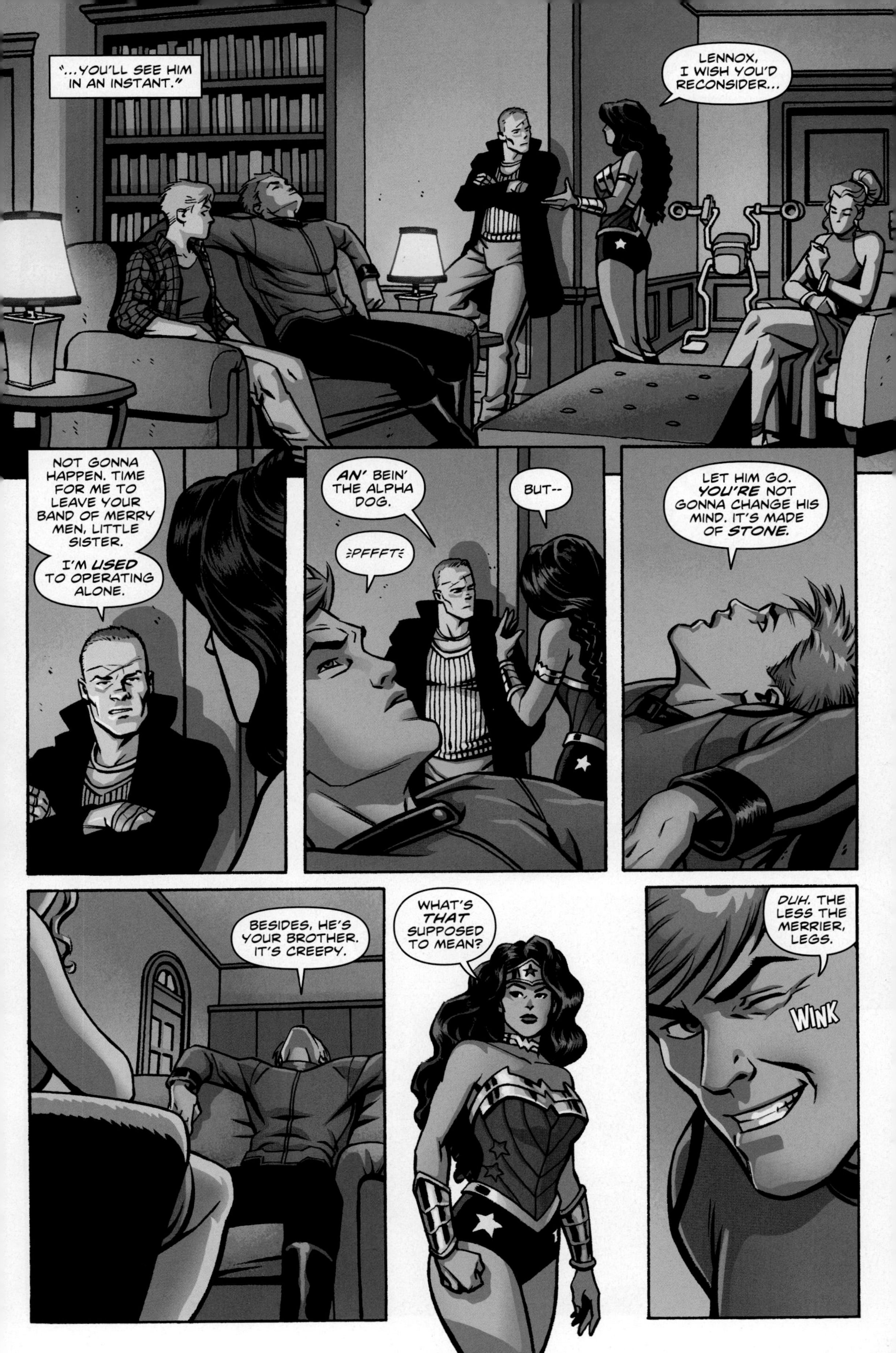
"...YOU'LL SEE HIM IN AN INSTANT."
LENNOX, I WISH YOU'D RECONSIDER...
NOT GONNA HAPPEN. TIME FOR ME TO LEAVE YOUR BAND OF MERRY MEN, LITTLE SISTER.
I'M USED TO OPERATING ALONE.
AN' BEIN' THE ALPHA DOG.
PFFFT
BUT--
LET HIM GO. YOU'RE NOT GONNA CHANGE HIS MIND. IT'S MADE OF STONE.
BESIDES, HE'S YOUR BROTHER. IT'S CREEPY.
WHAT'S THAT SUPPOSED TO MEAN?
DUH. THE LESS THE MERRIER, LEGS.
WINK

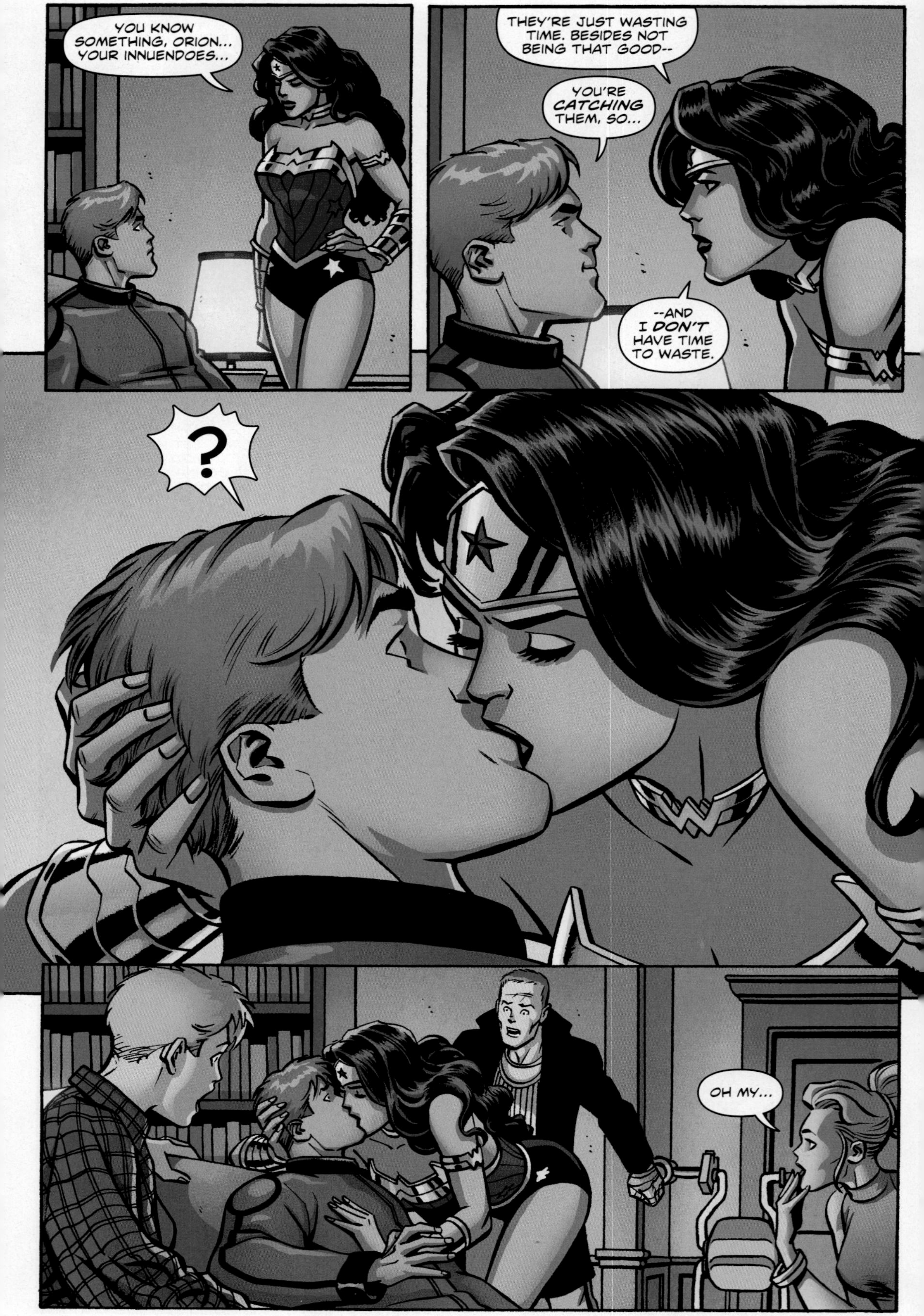
YOU KNOW SOMETHING, ORION... YOUR INNUENDOES...
THEY'RE JUST WASTING TIME. BESIDES NOT BEING THAT GOOD--
YOU'RE CATCHING THEM, SO...
--AND I DON'T HAVE TIME TO WASTE.
?
OH MY...

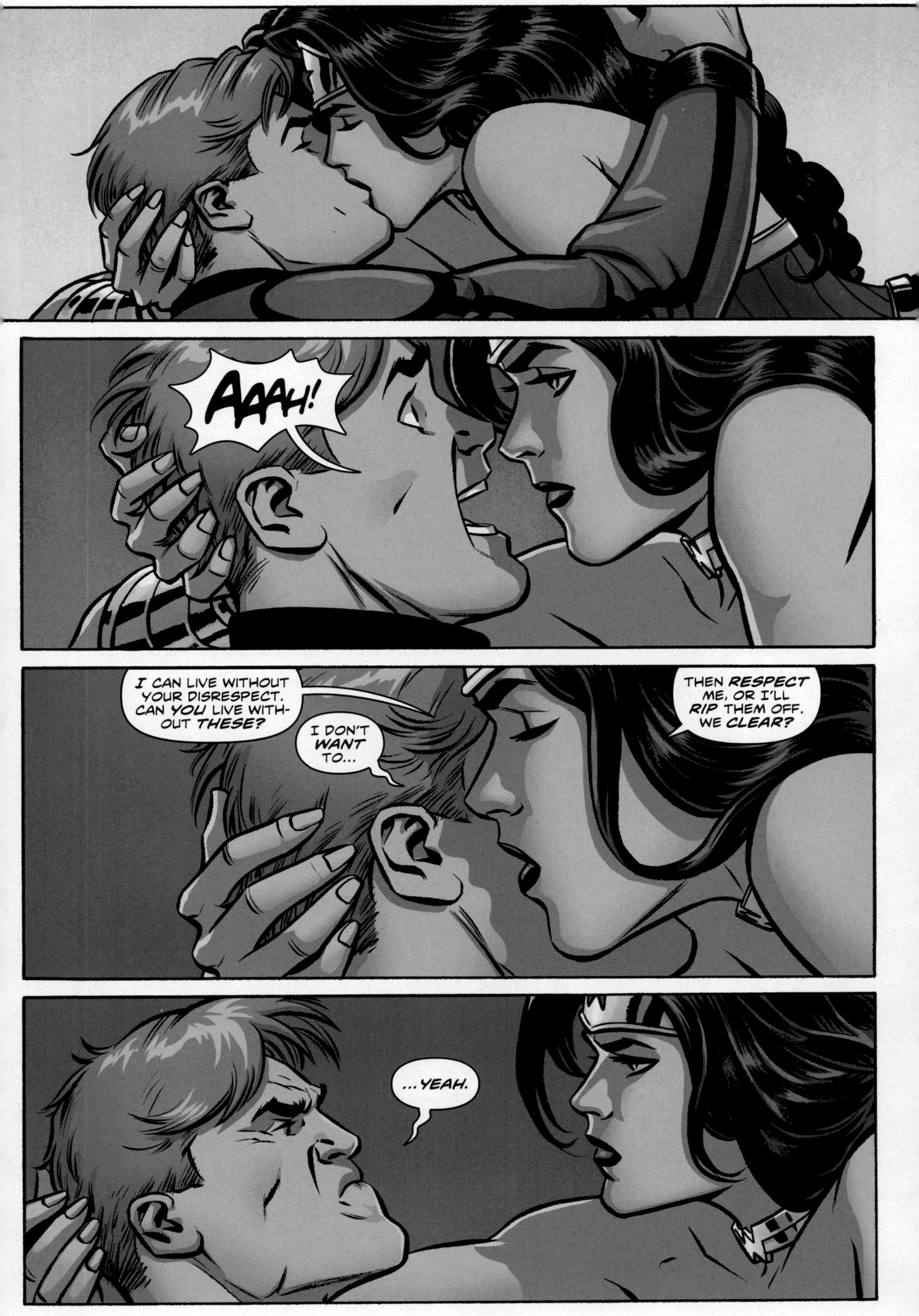
AAAH!
I CAN LIVE WITHOUT YOUR DISRESPECT. CAN YOU LIVE WITHOUT THESE?
I DON'T WANT TO...
THEN RESPECT ME, OR I'LL RIP THEM OFF. WE CLEAR?
...YEAH.

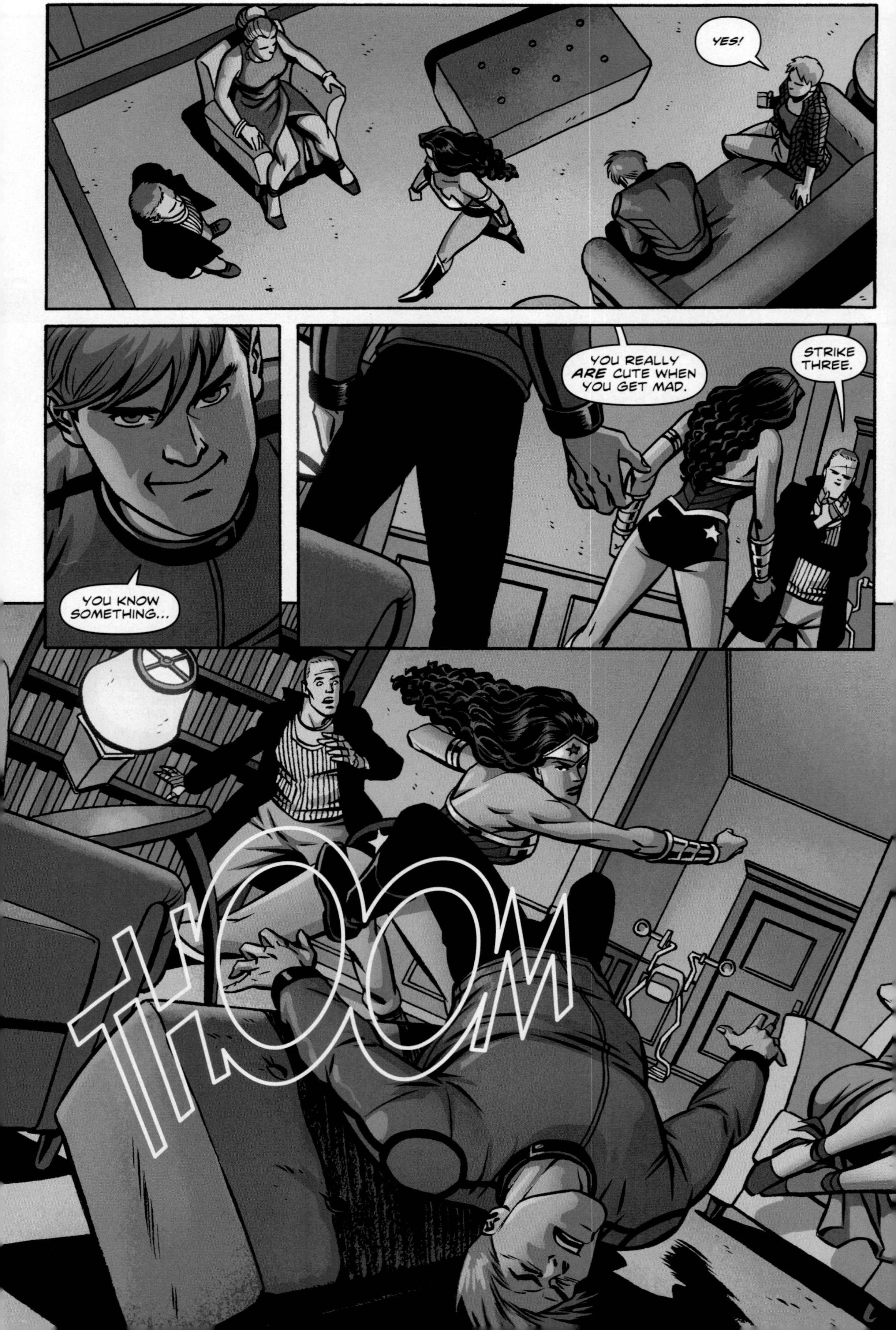
YES!
YOU KNOW SOMETHING...
YOU REALLY ARE CUTE WHEN YOU GET MAD.
STRIKE THREE.
THOOM

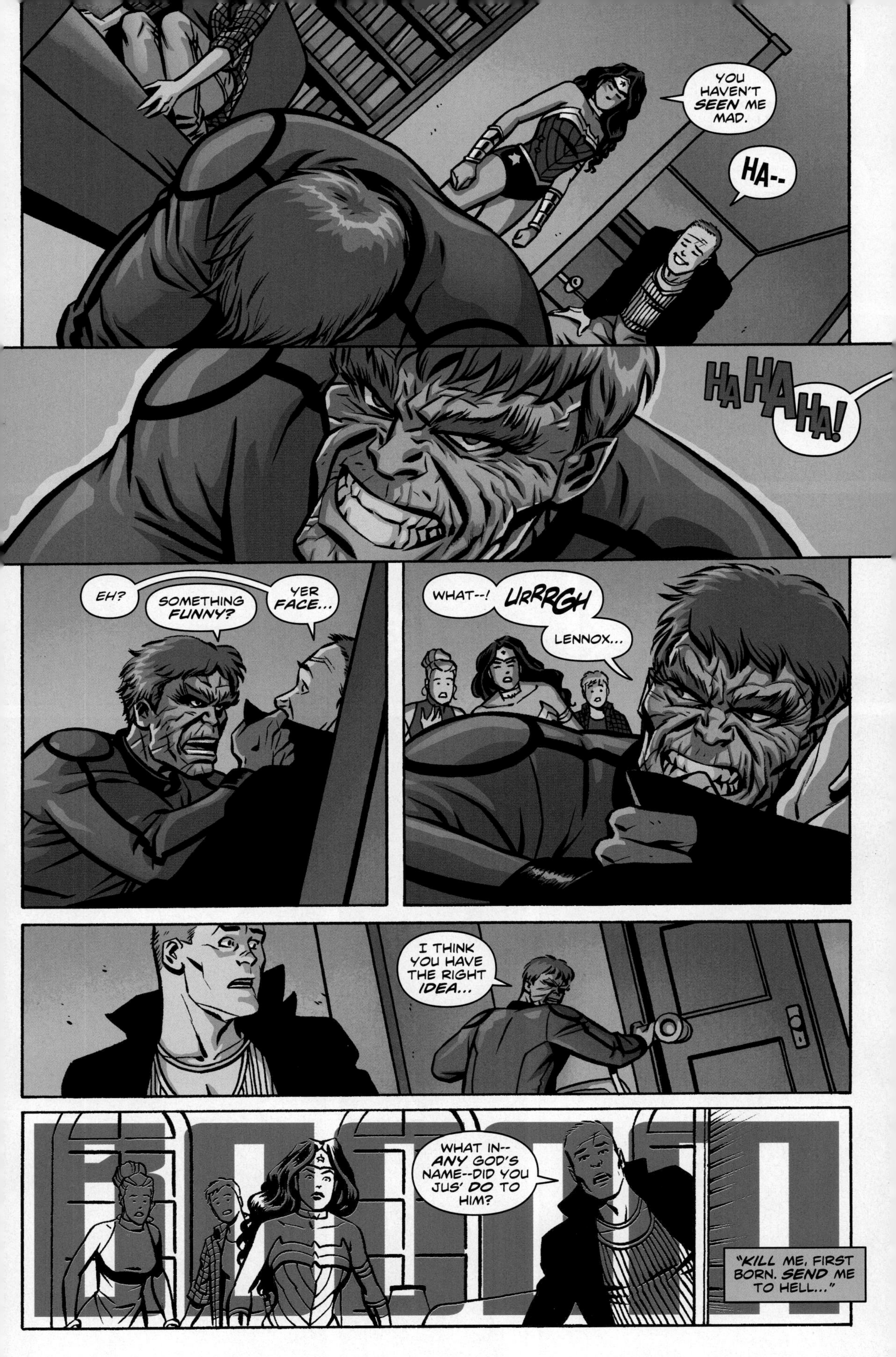
YOU HAVEN'T SEEN ME MAD.
HA--
HA HA HA HA!
EH?
SOMETHING FUNNY?
YER FACE...
WHAT--!
URRRGH
LENNOX...
I THINK YOU HAVE THE RIGHT IDEA...
WHAT IN-- ANY GOD'S NAME--DID YOU JUS' DO TO HIM?
"KILL ME, FIRST BORN. SEND ME TO HELL..."

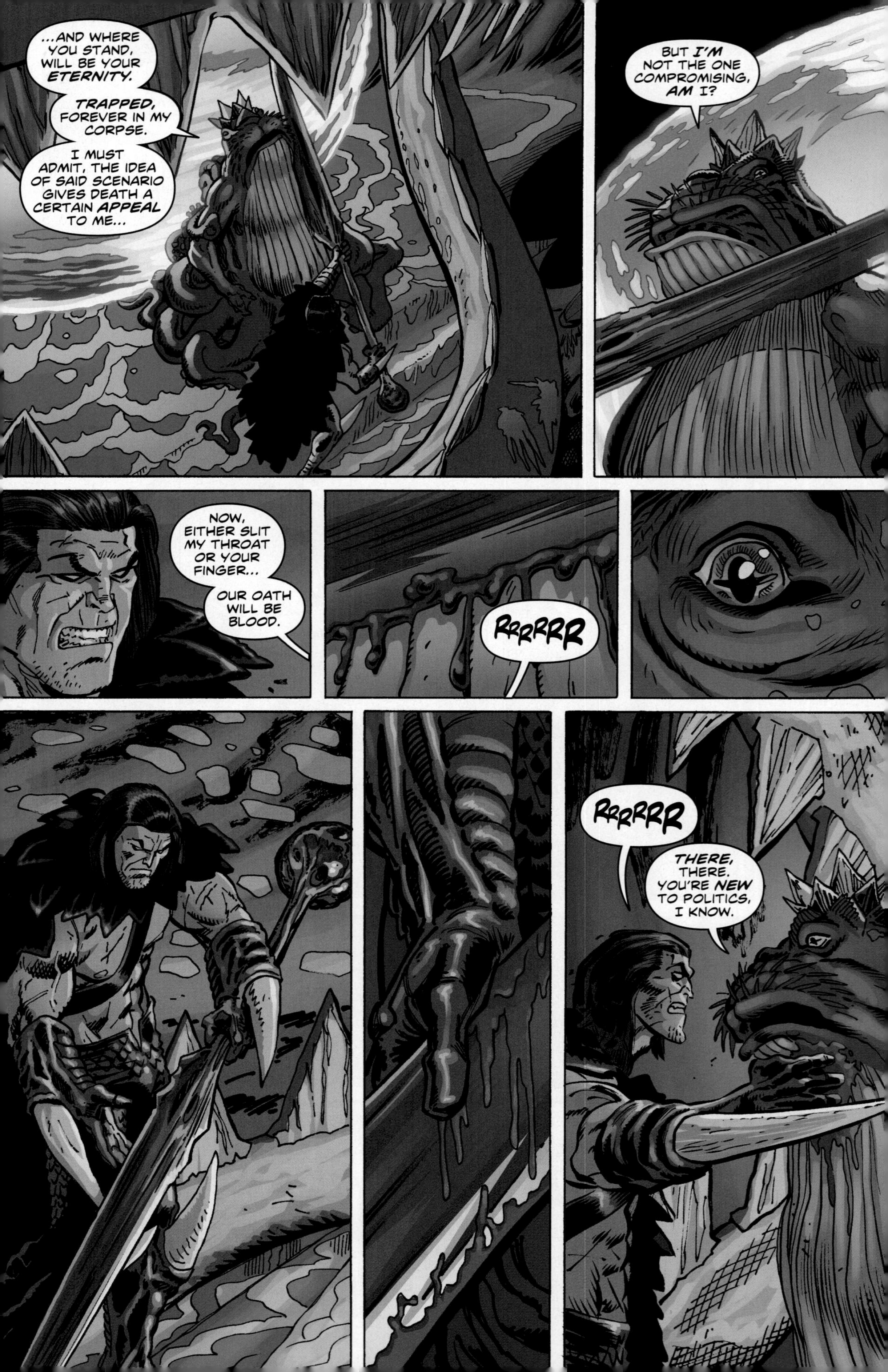
...AND WHERE YOU STAND, WILL BE YOUR ETERNITY.
TRAPPED, FOREVER IN MY CORPSE.
I MUST ADMIT, THE IDEA OF SAID SCENARIO GIVES DEATH A CERTAIN APPEAL TO ME...
BUT I'M NOT THE ONE COMPROMISING, AM I?
NOW, EITHER SLIT MY THROAT OR YOUR FINGER...
OUR OATH WILL BE BLOOD.
RRRRRR
RRRRRR
THERE, THERE. YOU'RE NEW TO POLITICS, I KNOW.

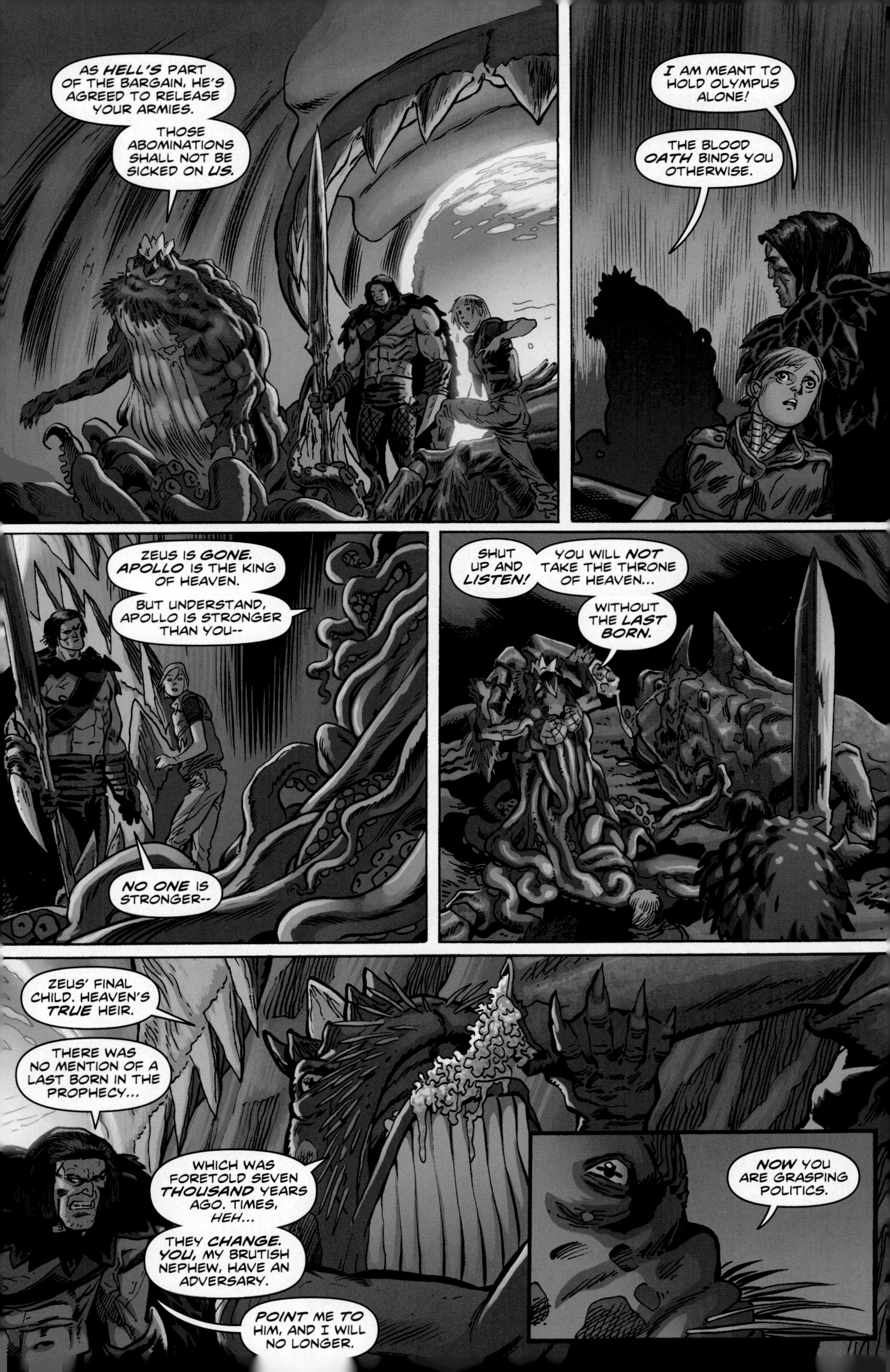

AS HELL'S PART OF THE BARGAIN, HE'S AGREED TO RELEASE YOUR ARMIES.
THOSE ABOMINATIONS SHALL NOT BE SICKED ON US.
I AM MEANT TO HOLD OLYMPUS ALONE!
THE BLOOD OATH BINDS YOU OTHERWISE.
ZEUS IS GONE. APOLLO IS THE KING OF HEAVEN.
BUT UNDERSTAND, APOLLO IS STRONGER THAN YOU--
NO ONE IS STRONGER--
SHUT UP AND LISTEN!
YOU WILL NOT TAKE THE THRONE OF HEAVEN...
WITHOUT THE LAST BORN.
ZEUS' FINAL CHILD. HEAVEN'S TRUE HEIR.
THERE WAS NO MENTION OF A LAST BORN IN THE PROPHECY...
WHICH WAS FORETOLD SEVEN THOUSAND YEARS AGO. TIMES, HEH...
THEY CHANGE. YOU, MY BRUTISH NEPHEW, HAVE AN ADVERSARY.
POINT ME TO HIM, AND I WILL NO LONGER.
NOW YOU ARE GRASPING POLITICS.

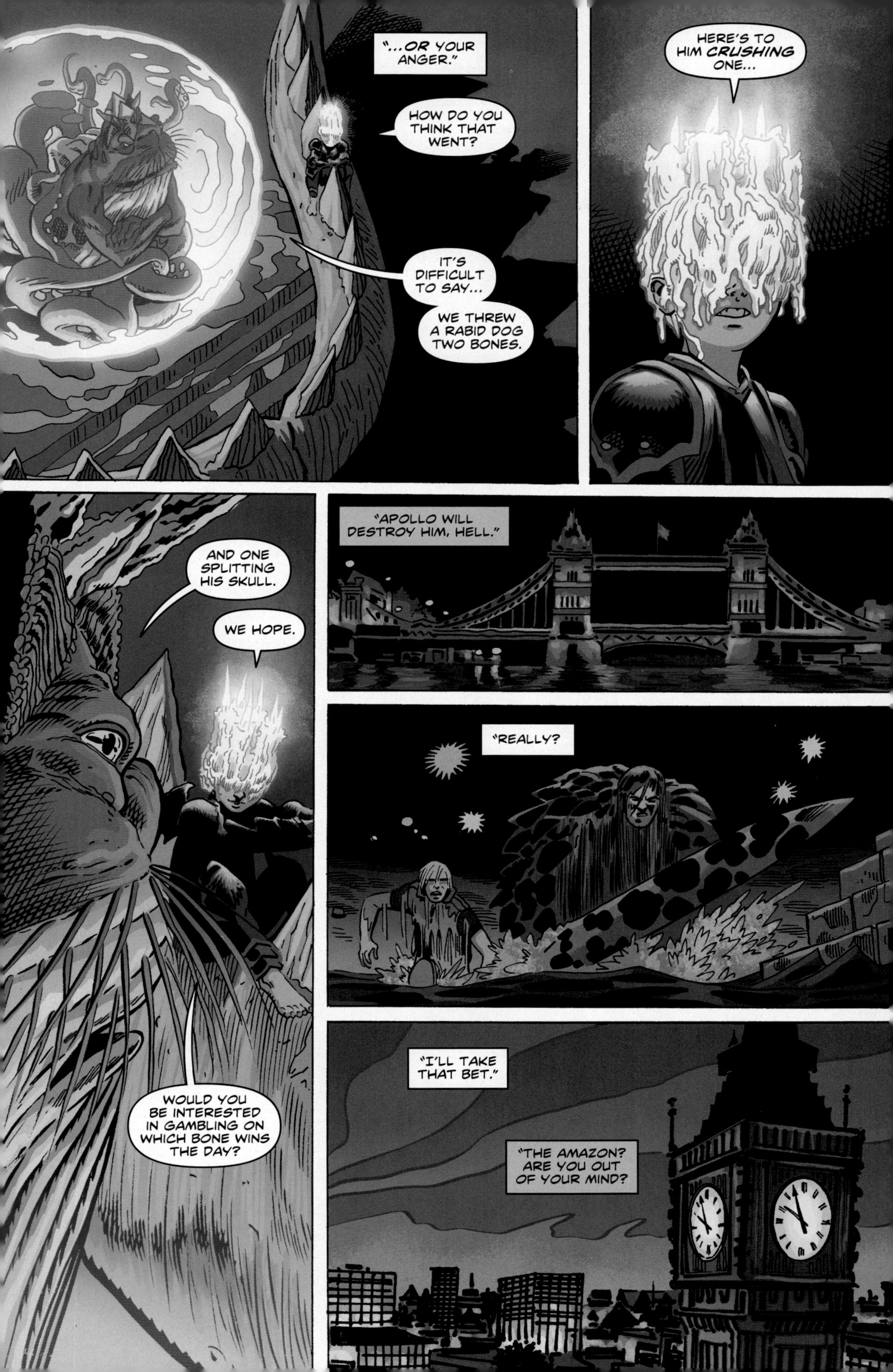
"...OR YOUR ANGER."
HOW DO YOU THINK THAT WENT?
IT'S DIFFICULT TO SAY...
WE THREW A RABID DOG TWO BONES.
HERE'S TO HIM CRUSHING ONE...
AND ONE SPLITTING HIS SKULL.
WE HOPE.
WOULD YOU BE INTERESTED IN GAMBLING ON WHICH BONE WINS THE DAY?
"APOLLO WILL DESTROY HIM, HELL."
"REALLY?
"I'LL TAKE THAT BET."
"THE AMAZON? ARE YOU OUT OF YOUR MIND?

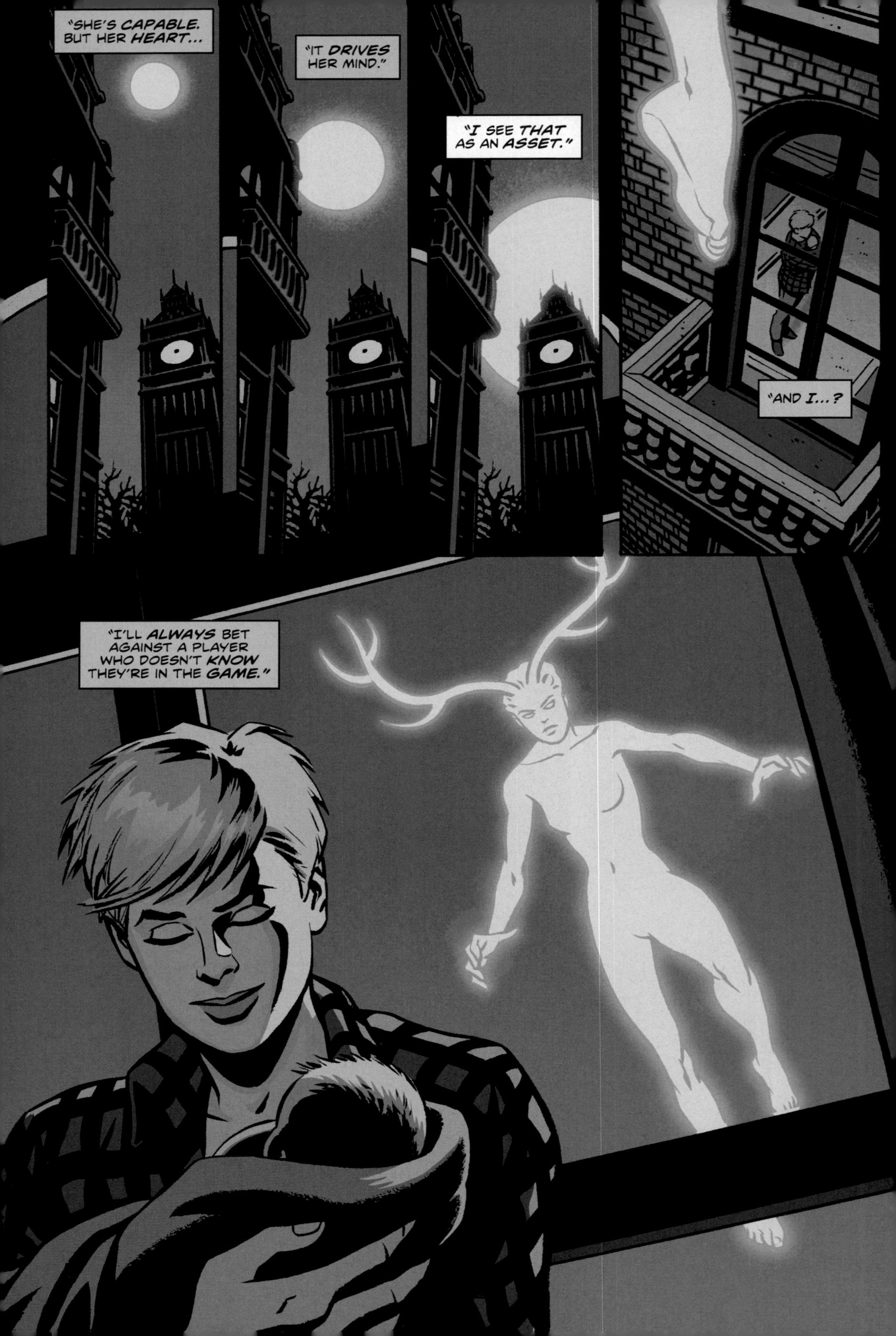
"SHE'S CAPABLE. BUT HER HEART...
"IT DRIVES HER MIND."
"I SEE THAT AS AN ASSET."
"AND I...?
"I'LL ALWAYS BET AGAINST A PLAYER WHO DOESN'T KNOW THEY'RE IN THE GAME."

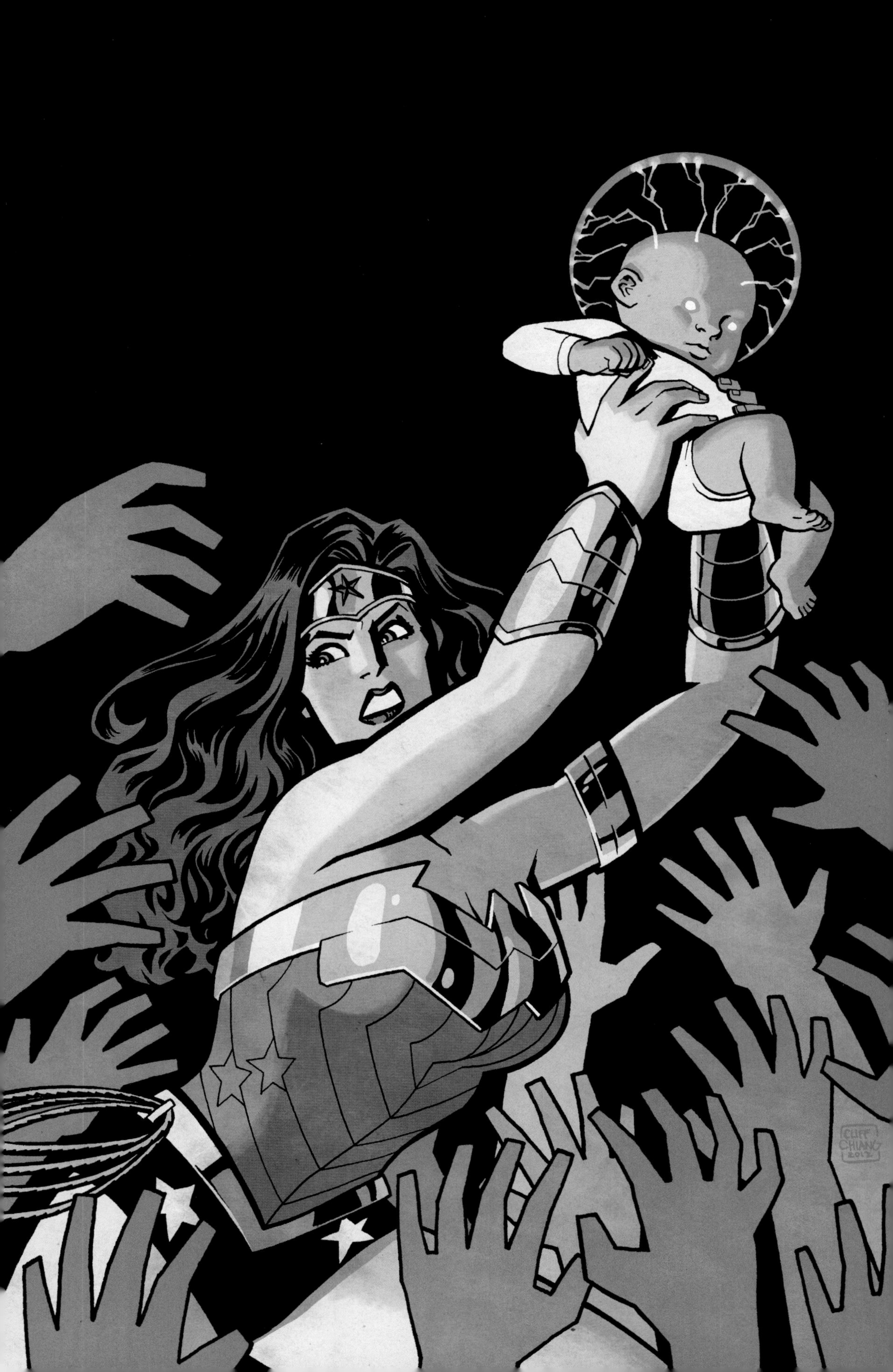
CLIFF CHIANG 2012

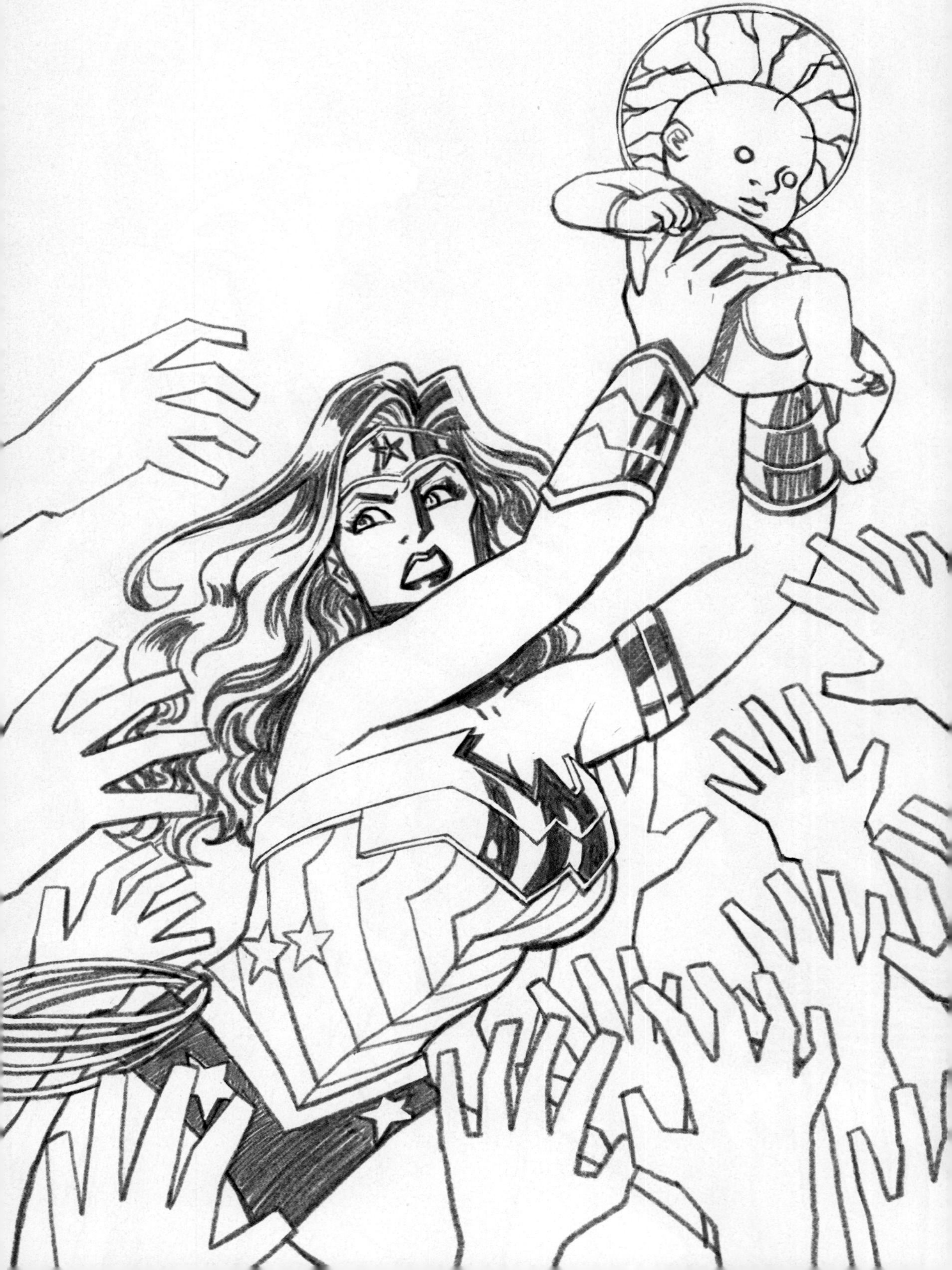

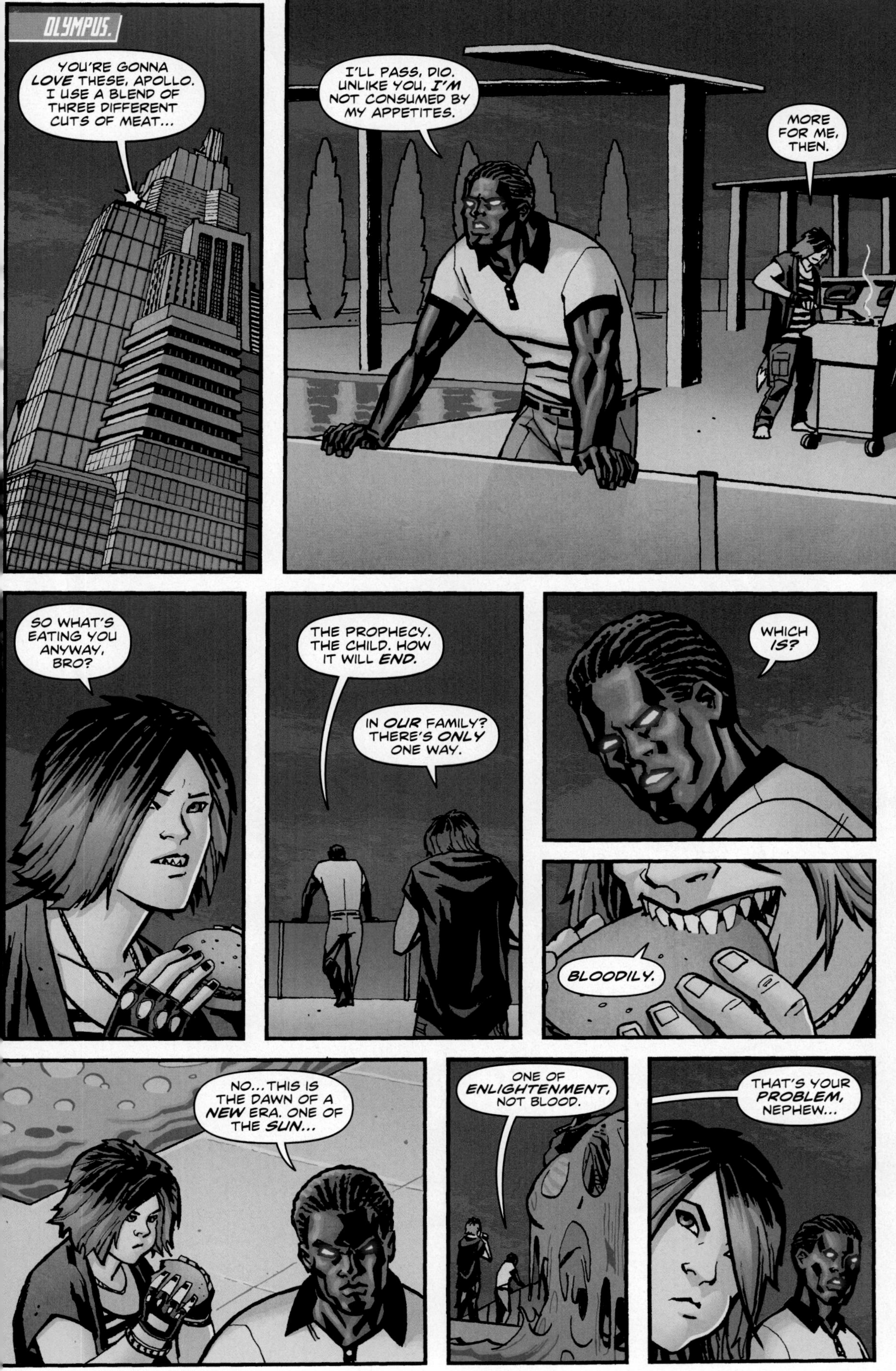
OLYMPUS.
YOU'RE GONNA LOVE THESE, APOLLO. I USE A BLEND OF THREE DIFFERENT CUTS OF MEAT...
I'LL PASS, DIO. UNLIKE YOU, I'M NOT CONSUMED BY MY APPETITES.
MORE FOR ME, THEN.
SO WHAT'S EATING YOU ANYWAY, BRO?
THE PROPHECY. THE CHILD. HOW IT WILL END.
IN OUR FAMILY? THERE'S ONLY ONE WAY.
WHICH IS?
BLOODILY.
NO...THIS IS THE DAWN OF A NEW ERA. ONE OF THE SUN...
ONE OF ENLIGHTENMENT, NOT BLOOD.
THAT'S YOUR PROBLEM, NEPHEW...

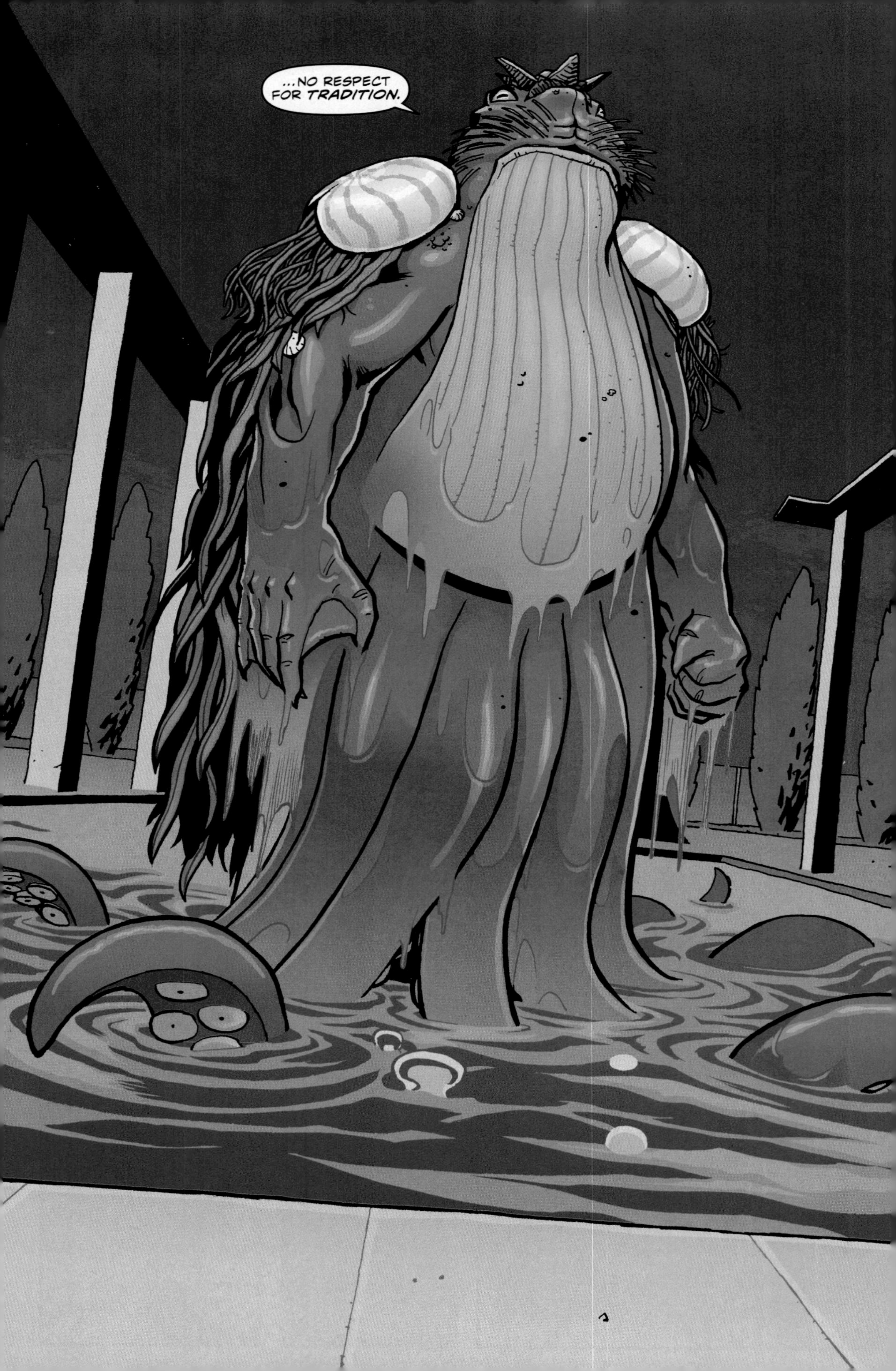
...NO RESPECT FOR TRADITION.

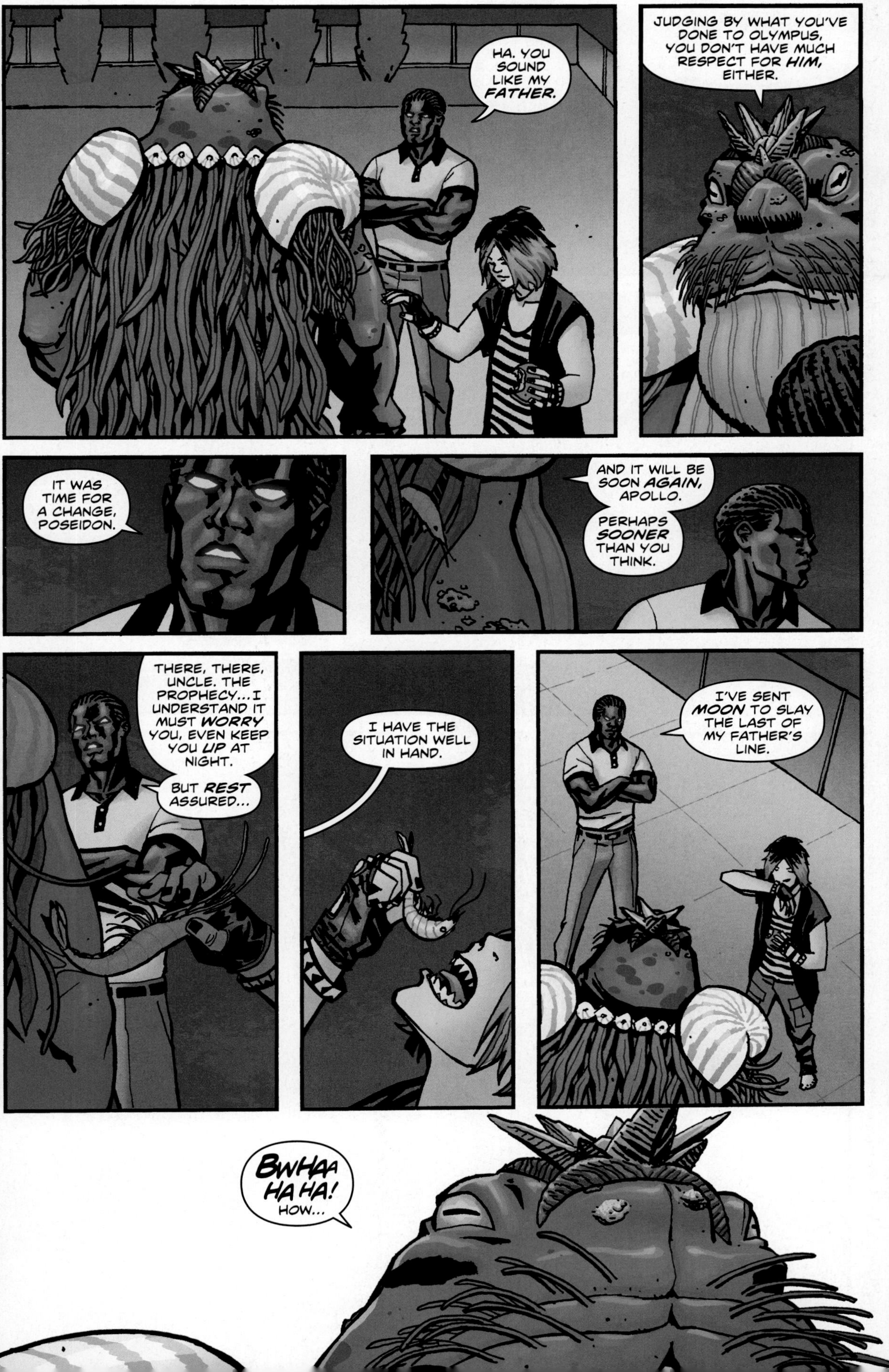
HA. YOU SOUND LIKE MY FATHER.
JUDGING BY WHAT YOU'VE DONE TO OLYMPUS, YOU DON'T HAVE MUCH RESPECT FOR HIM, EITHER.
IT WAS TIME FOR A CHANGE, POSEIDON.
AND IT WILL BE SOON AGAIN, APOLLO.
PERHAPS SOONER THAN YOU THINK.
THERE, THERE, UNCLE. THE PROPHECY... I UNDERSTAND IT MUST WORRY YOU, EVEN KEEP YOU UP AT NIGHT.
BUT REST ASSURED...
I HAVE THE SITUATION WELL IN HAND.
I'VE SENT MOON TO SLAY THE LAST OF MY FATHER'S LINE.
BWHAA HA HA! HOW...

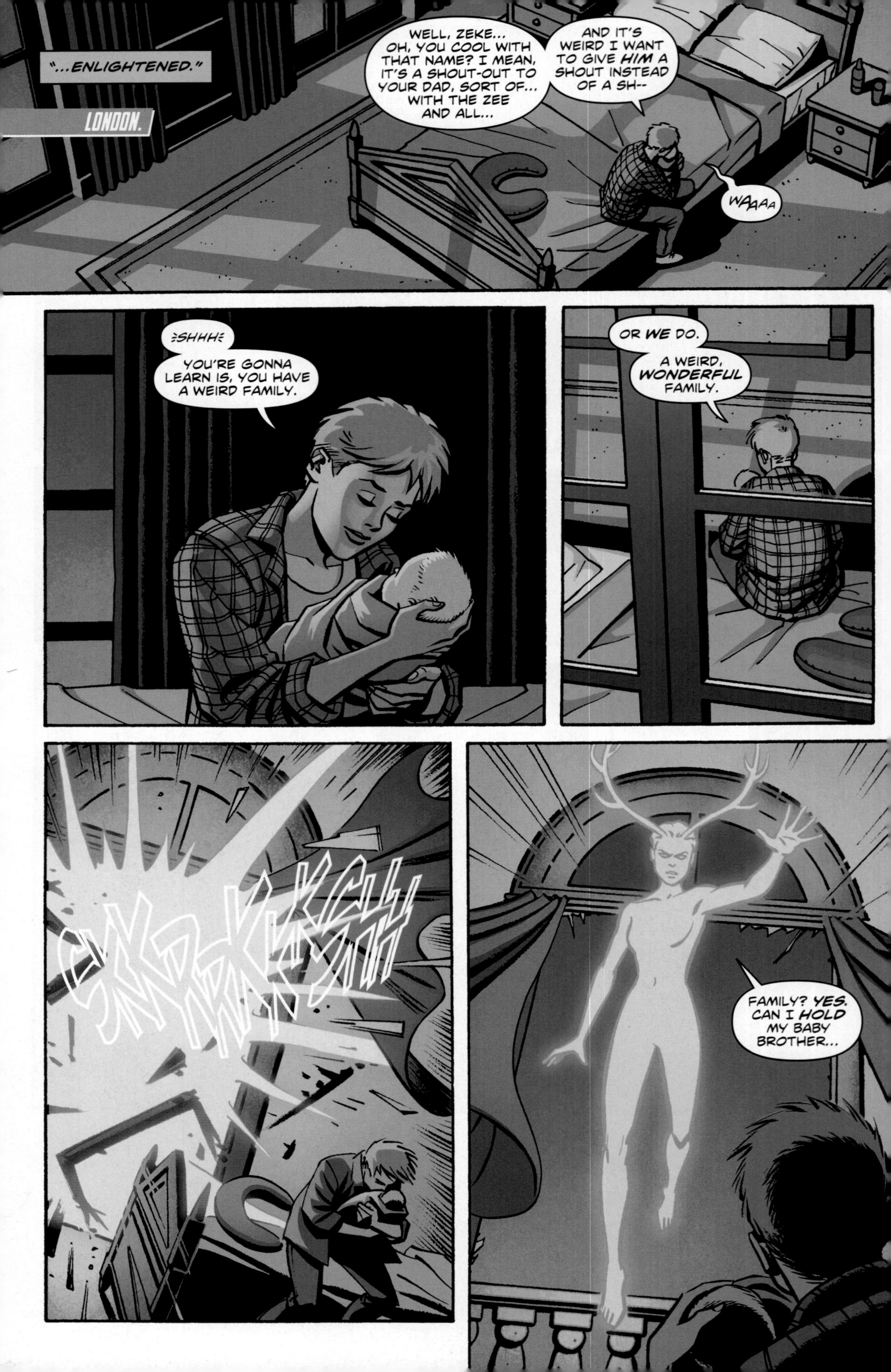
"...ENLIGHTENED."
LONDON.
WELL, ZEKE... OH, YOU COOL WITH THAT NAME? I MEAN, IT'S A SHOUT-OUT TO YOUR DAD, SORT OF... WITH THE ZEE AND ALL...
AND IT'S WEIRD I WANT TO GIVE HIM A SHOUT INSTEAD OF A SH--
WAAAA
SHHH
YOU'RE GONNA LEARN IS, YOU HAVE A WEIRD FAMILY.
OR WE DO.
A WEIRD, WONDERFUL FAMILY.
CHKRKKCHH
FAMILY? YES. CAN I HOLD MY BABY BROTHER...

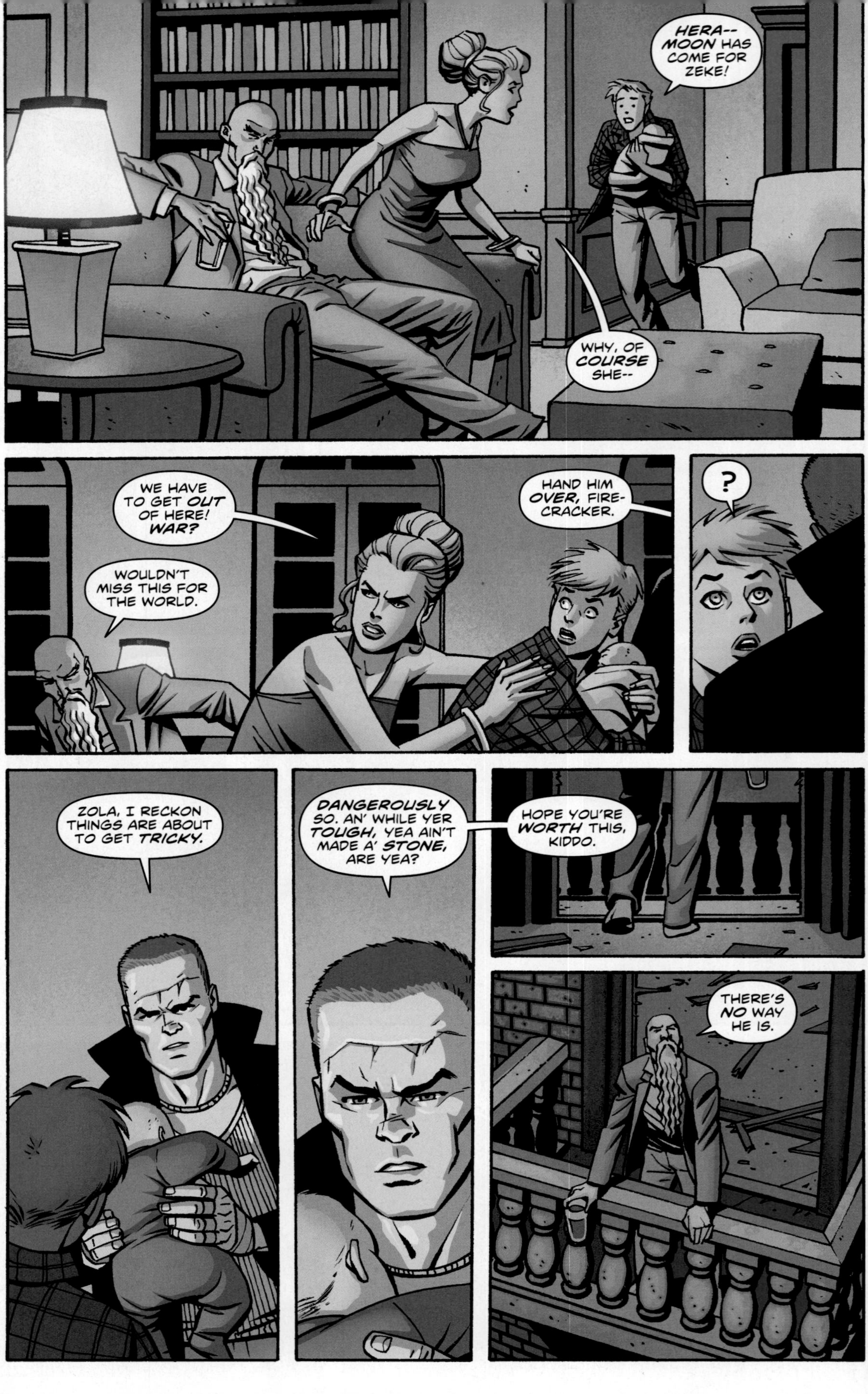

HERA--
MOON HAS COME FOR ZEKE!
WHY, OF COURSE SHE--
WE HAVE TO GET OUT OF HERE! WAR?
WOULDN'T MISS THIS FOR THE WORLD.
HAND HIM OVER, FIRE-CRACKER.
?
ZOLA, I RECKON THINGS ARE ABOUT TO GET TRICKY.
DANGEROUSLY SO. AN' WHILE YER TOUGH, YEA AIN'T MADE A' STONE, ARE YEA?
HOPE YOU'RE WORTH THIS, KIDDO.
THERE'S NO WAY HE IS.

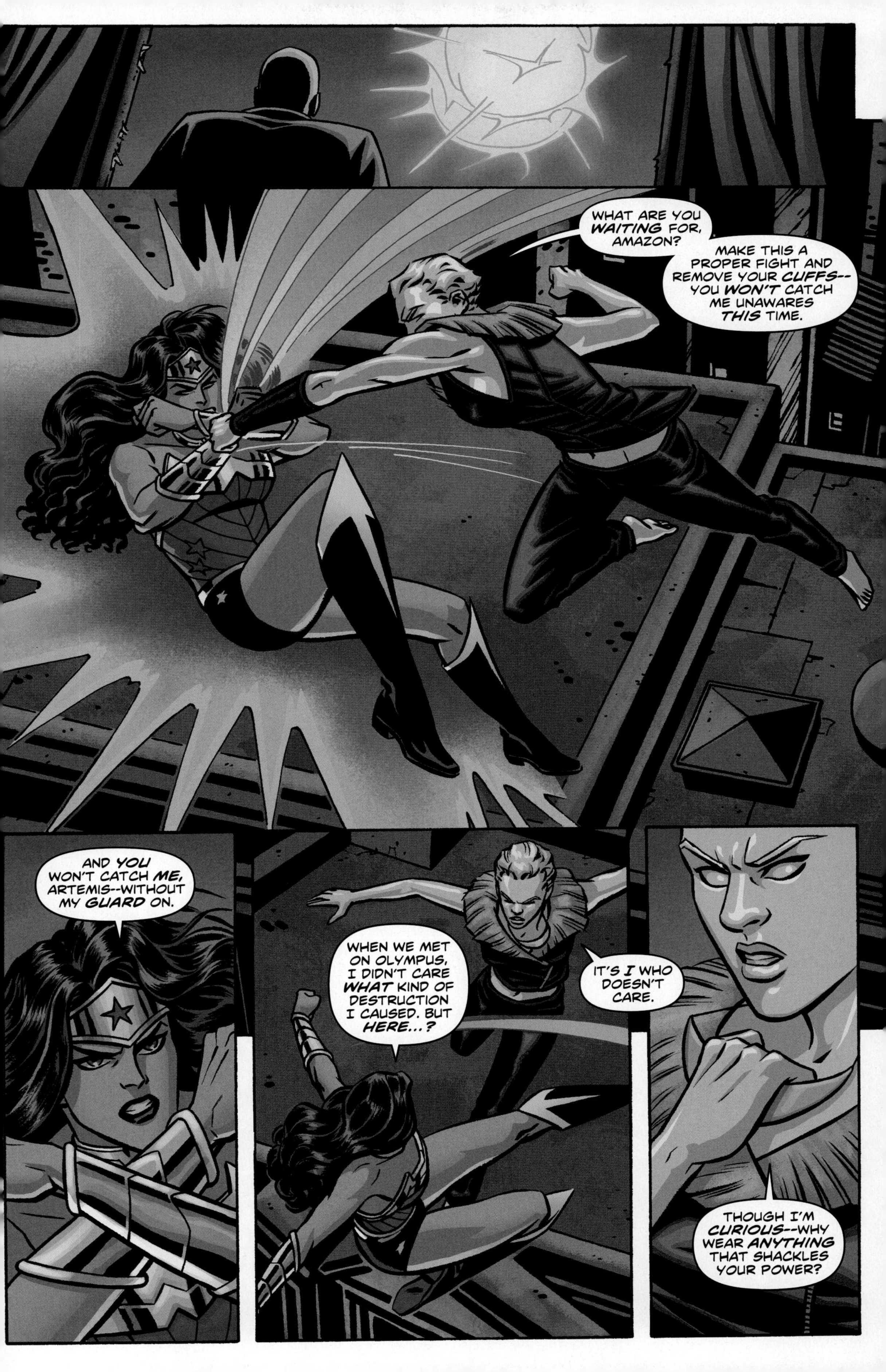
WHAT ARE YOU WAITING FOR, AMAZON?
MAKE THIS A PROPER FIGHT AND REMOVE YOUR CUFFS--YOU WON'T CATCH ME UNAWARES THIS TIME.
AND YOU WON'T CATCH ME, ARTEMIS--WITHOUT MY GUARD ON.
WHEN WE MET ON OLYMPUS, I DIDN'T CARE WHAT KIND OF DESTRUCTION I CAUSED. BUT HERE...?
IT'S I WHO DOESN'T CARE.
THOUGH I'M CURIOUS--WHY WEAR ANYTHING THAT SHACKLES YOUR POWER?

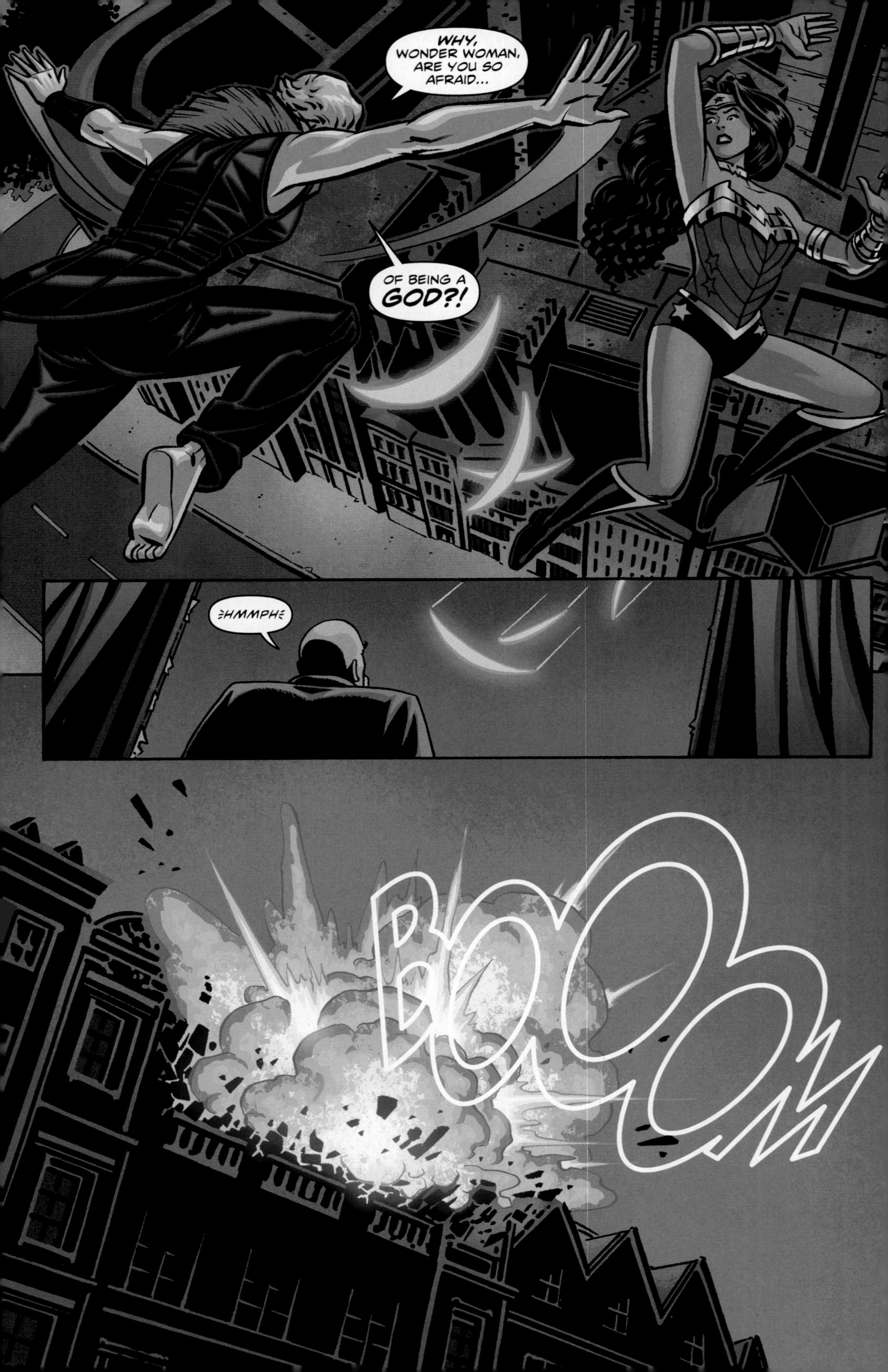
WHY, WONDER WOMAN, ARE YOU SO AFRAID...
OF BEING A GOD?!
HMMPH
BOOOOM

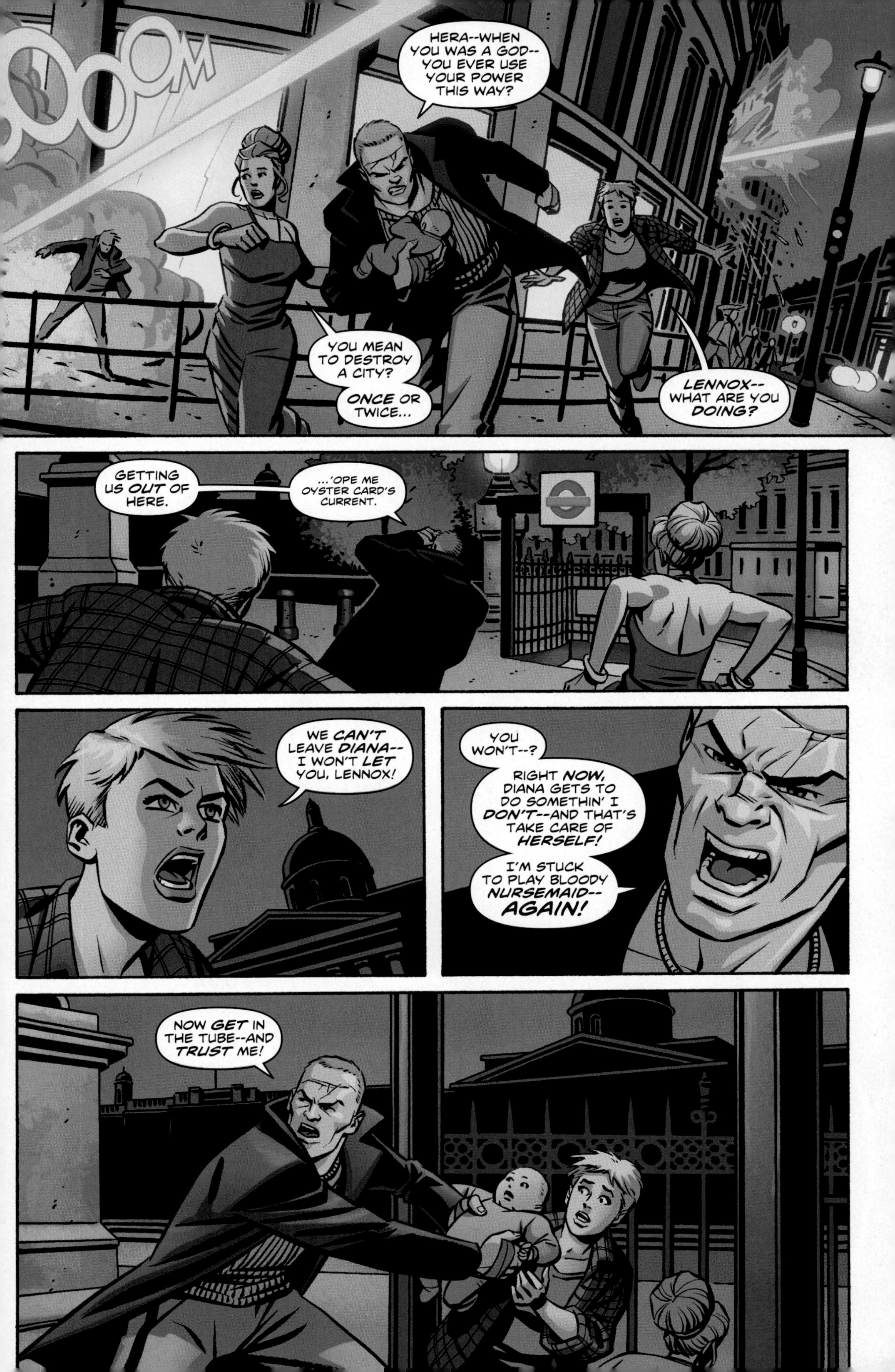
BOOOM
HERA--WHEN YOU WAS A GOD--YOU EVER USE YOUR POWER THIS WAY?
YOU MEAN TO DESTROY A CITY?
ONCE OR TWICE...
LENNOX--WHAT ARE YOU DOING?
GETTING US OUT OF HERE.
...'OPE ME OYSTER CARD'S CURRENT.
WE CAN'T LEAVE DIANA--I WON'T LET YOU, LENNOX!
YOU WON'T--?
RIGHT NOW, DIANA GETS TO DO SOMETHIN' I DON'T--AND THAT'S TAKE CARE OF HERSELF!
I'M STUCK TO PLAY BLOODY NURSEMAID--AGAIN!
NOW GET IN THE TUBE--AND TRUST ME!

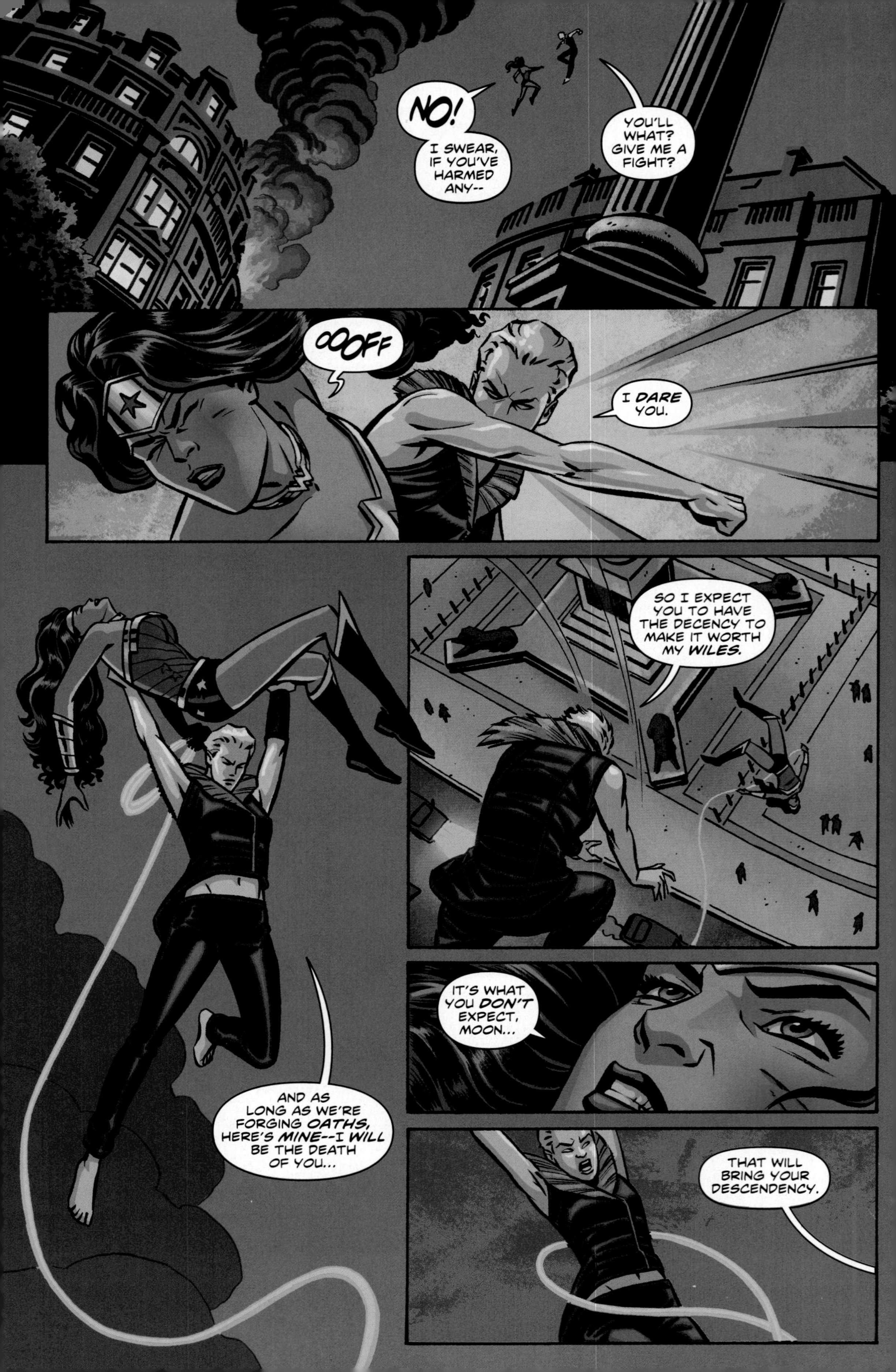
NO!
I SWEAR, IF YOU'VE HARMED ANY--
YOU'LL WHAT? GIVE ME A FIGHT?
OOOFF
I DARE YOU.
SO I EXPECT YOU TO HAVE THE DECENCY TO MAKE IT WORTH MY WILES.
AND AS LONG AS WE'RE FORGING OATHS, HERE'S MINE--I WILL BE THE DEATH OF YOU...
IT'S WHAT YOU DON'T EXPECT, MOON...
THAT WILL BRING YOUR DESCENDENCY.

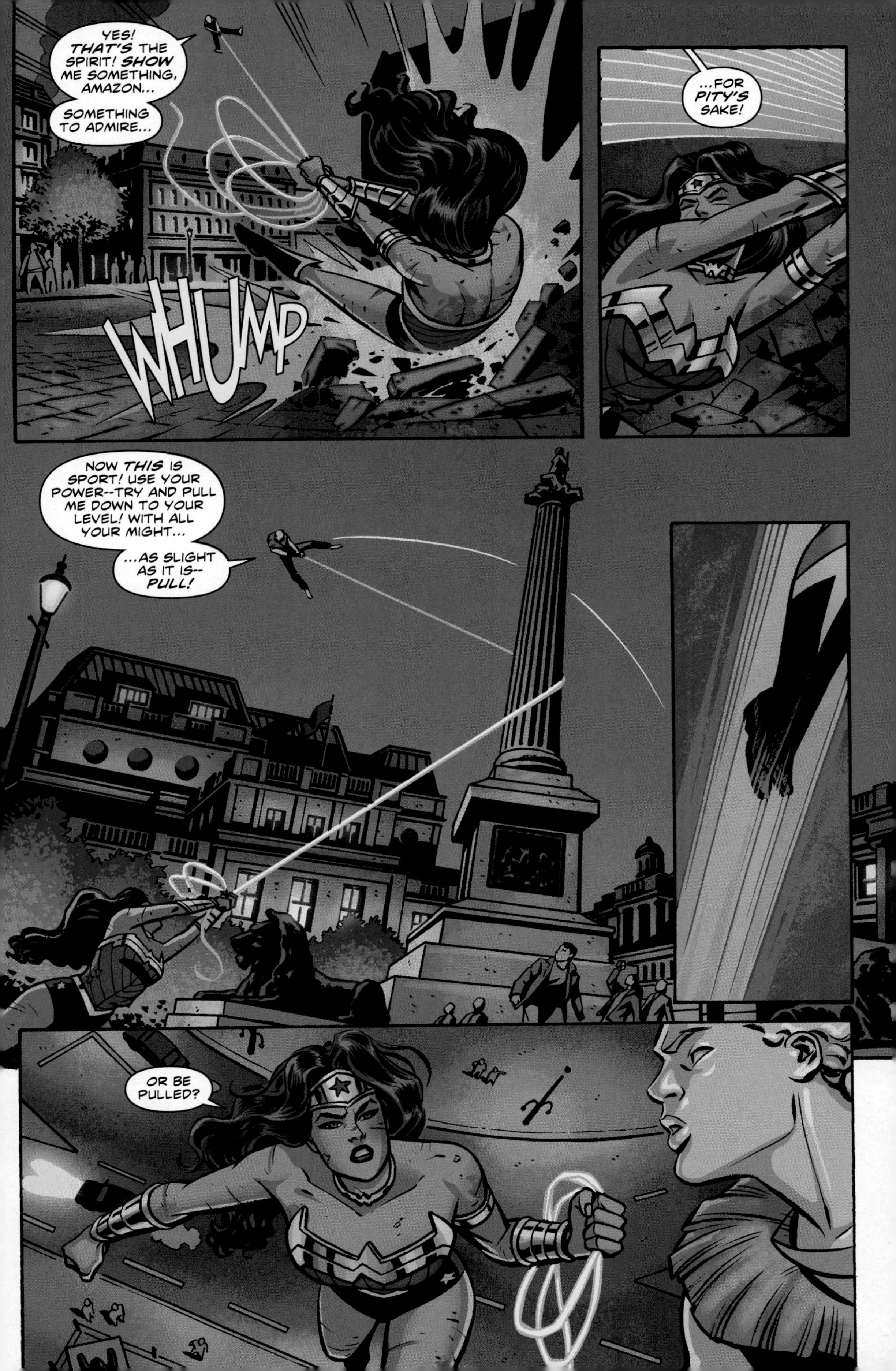
YES! THAT'S THE SPIRIT! SHOW ME SOMETHING, AMAZON...
SOMETHING TO ADMIRE...
WHUMP
...FOR PITY'S SAKE!
NOW THIS IS SPORT! USE YOUR POWER--TRY AND PULL ME DOWN TO YOUR LEVEL! WITH ALL YOUR MIGHT...
...AS SLIGHT AS IT IS--PULL!
OR BE PULLED?

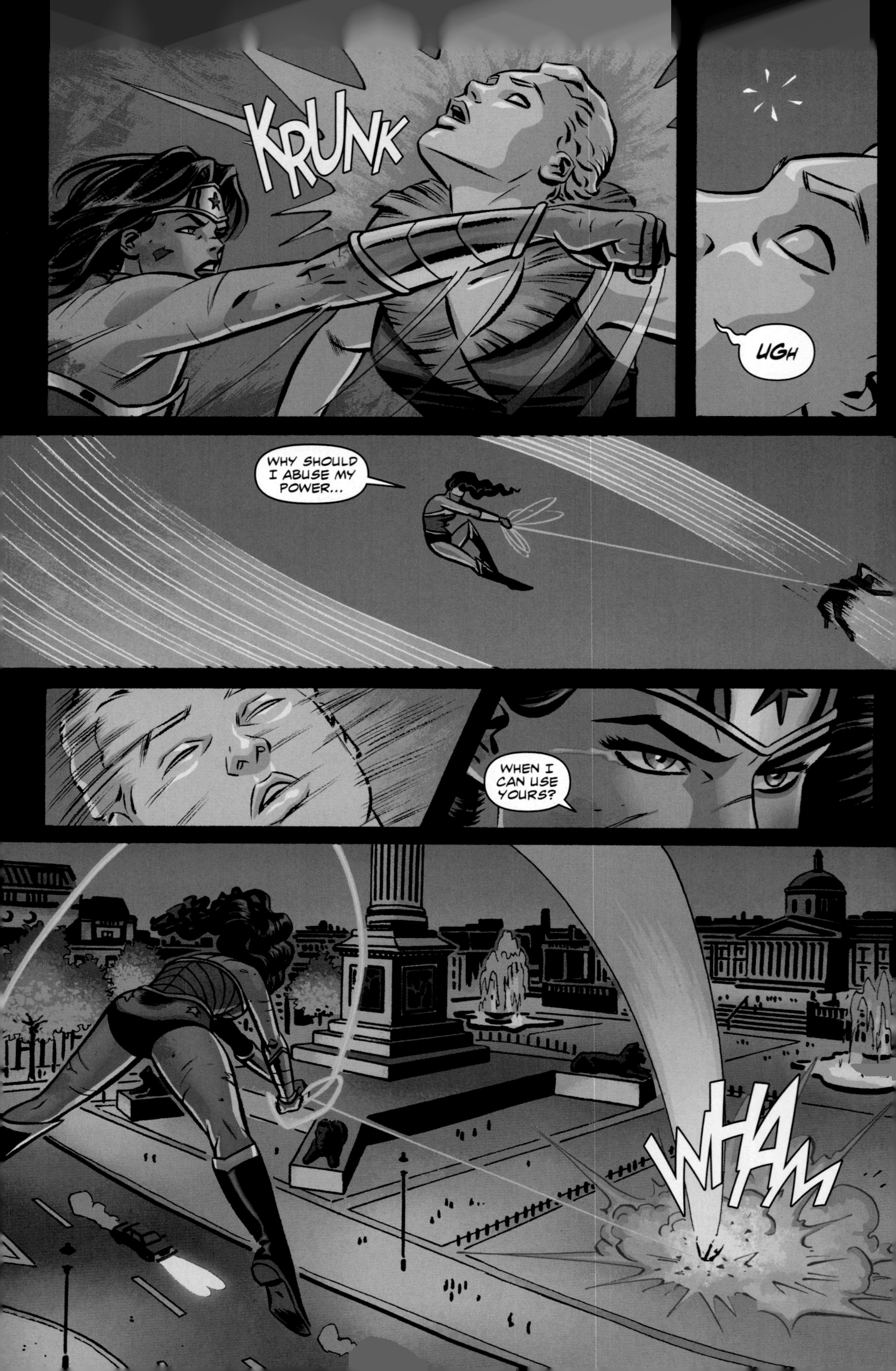
KRUNK
UGH
WHY SHOULD I ABUSE MY POWER...
WHEN I CAN USE YOURS?
WHAM

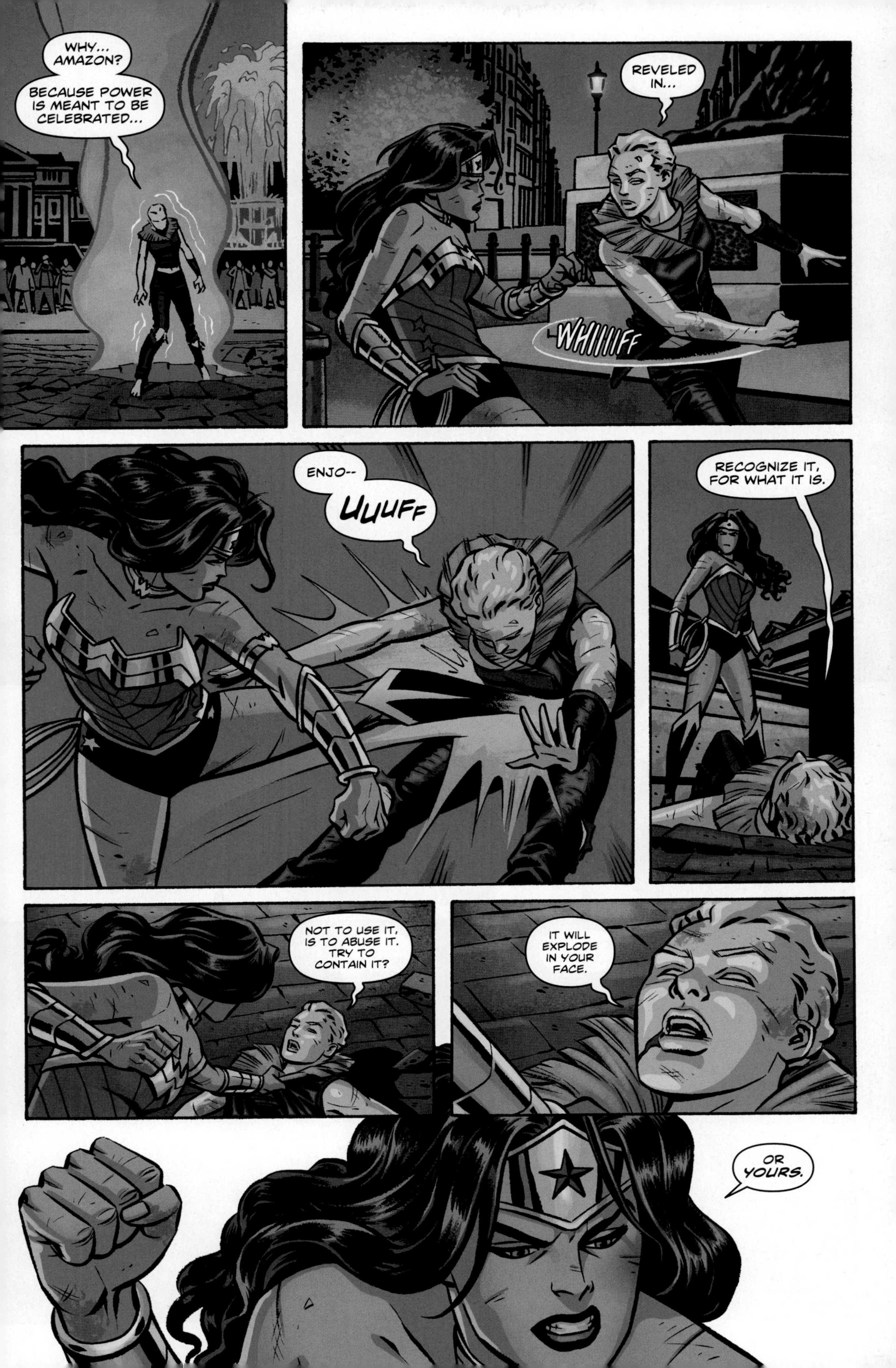
WHY... AMAZON?
BECAUSE POWER IS MEANT TO BE CELEBRATED...
REVELED IN...
WHIIIIFF
ENJO--
UUUFF
RECOGNIZE IT, FOR WHAT IT IS.
NOT TO USE IT, IS TO ABUSE IT. TRY TO CONTAIN IT?
IT WILL EXPLODE IN YOUR FACE.
OR YOURS.

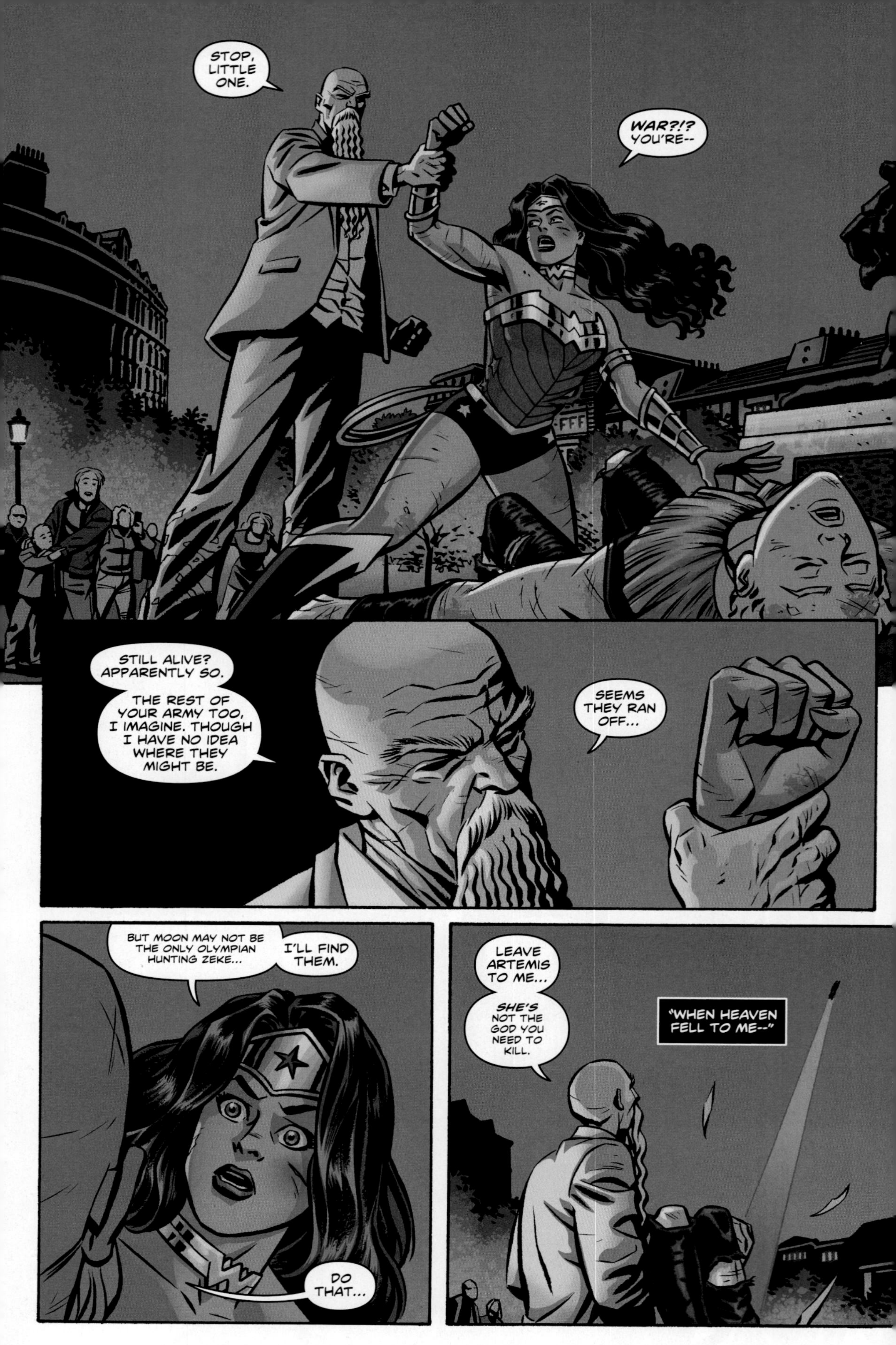

STOP, LITTLE ONE.
WAR?!? YOU'RE--
STILL ALIVE? APPARENTLY SO.
THE REST OF YOUR ARMY TOO, I IMAGINE. THOUGH I HAVE NO IDEA WHERE THEY MIGHT BE.
SEEMS THEY RAN OFF...
BUT MOON MAY NOT BE THE ONLY OLYMPIAN HUNTING ZEKE...
I'LL FIND THEM.
DO THAT...
LEAVE ARTEMIS TO ME...
SHE'S NOT THE GOD YOU NEED TO KILL.
"WHEN HEAVEN FELL TO ME--"

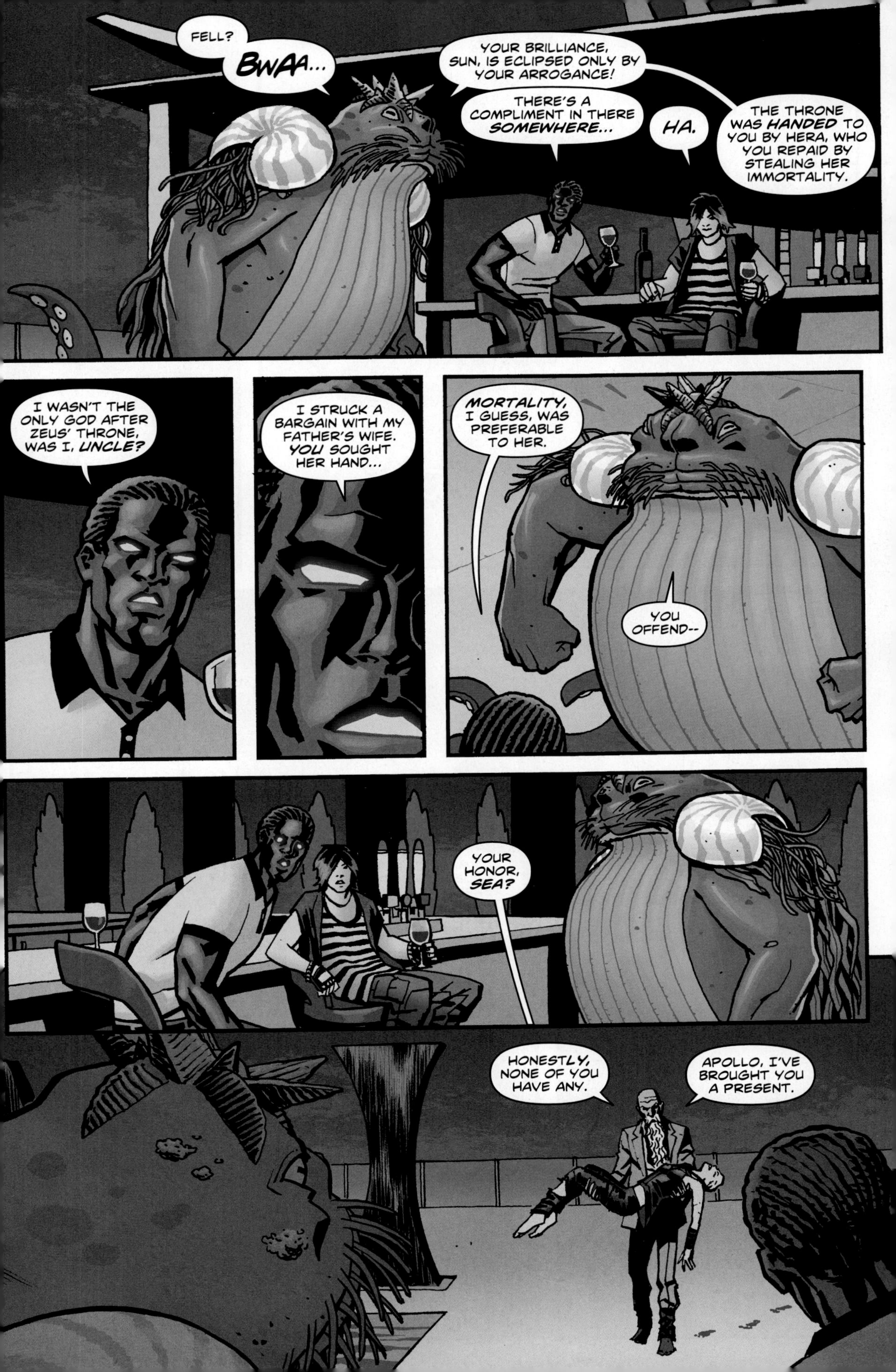
FELL? BWAA...
YOUR BRILLIANCE, SUN, IS ECLIPSED ONLY BY YOUR ARROGANCE!
THERE'S A COMPLIMENT IN THERE SOMEWHERE...
HA.
THE THRONE WAS HANDED TO YOU BY HERA, WHO YOU REPAID BY STEALING HER IMMORTALITY.
I WASN'T THE ONLY GOD AFTER ZEUS' THRONE, WAS I, UNCLE?
I STRUCK A BARGAIN WITH MY FATHER'S WIFE. YOU SOUGHT HER HAND...
MORTALITY, I GUESS, WAS PREFERABLE TO HER.
YOU OFFEND--
YOUR HONOR, SEA?
HONESTLY, NONE OF YOU HAVE ANY.
APOLLO, I'VE BROUGHT YOU A PRESENT.

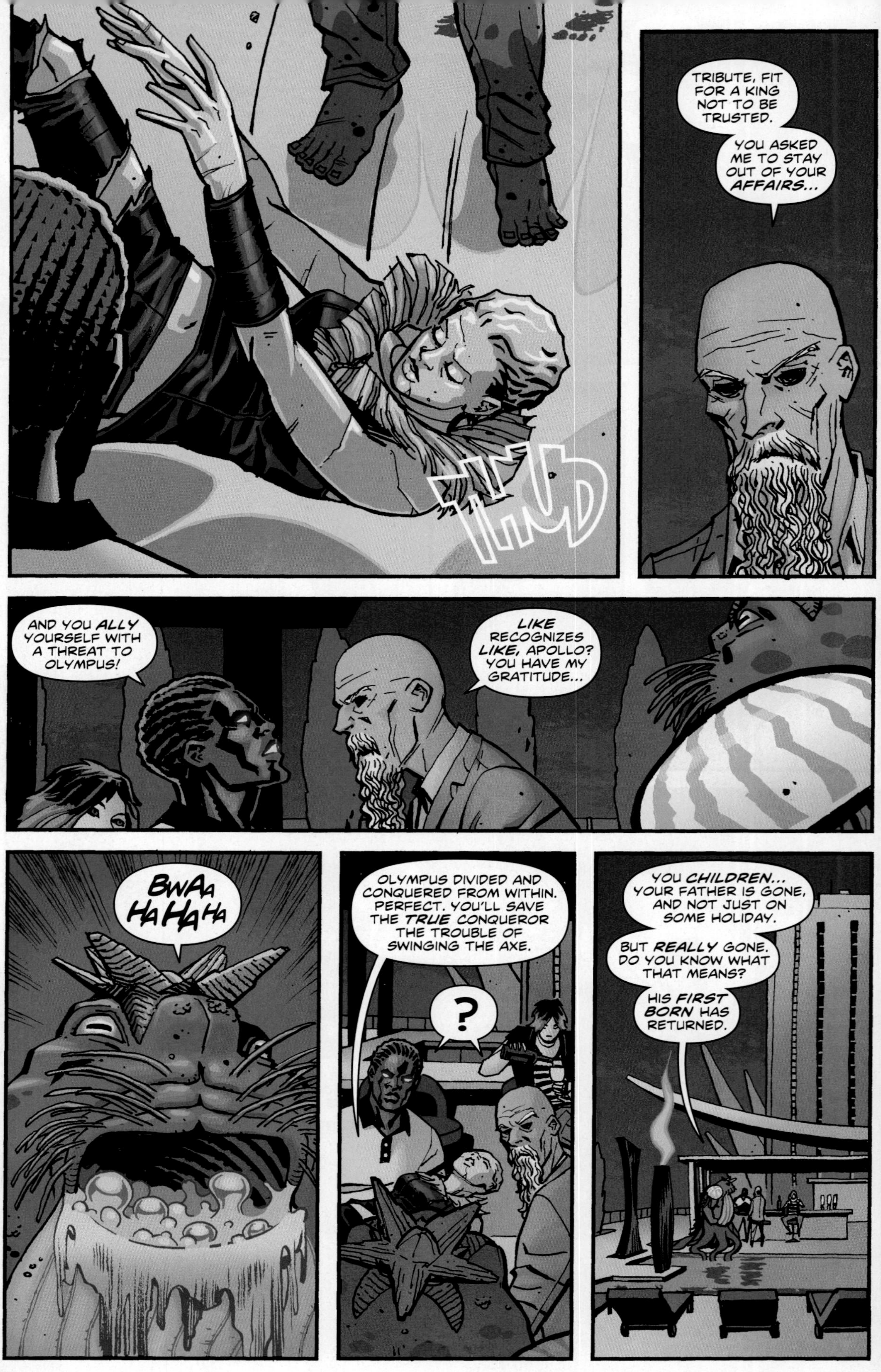
THUD
TRIBUTE, FIT FOR A KING NOT TO BE TRUSTED.
YOU ASKED ME TO STAY OUT OF YOUR AFFAIRS...
AND YOU ALLY YOURSELF WITH A THREAT TO OLYMPUS!
LIKE RECOGNIZES LIKE, APOLLO? YOU HAVE MY GRATITUDE...
BWAA HA HA HA HA
OLYMPUS DIVIDED AND CONQUERED FROM WITHIN. PERFECT. YOU'LL SAVE THE TRUE CONQUEROR THE TROUBLE OF SWINGING THE AXE.
?
YOU CHILDREN... YOUR FATHER IS GONE, AND NOT JUST ON SOME HOLIDAY.
BUT REALLY GONE. DO YOU KNOW WHAT THAT MEANS?
HIS FIRST BORN HAS RETURNED.

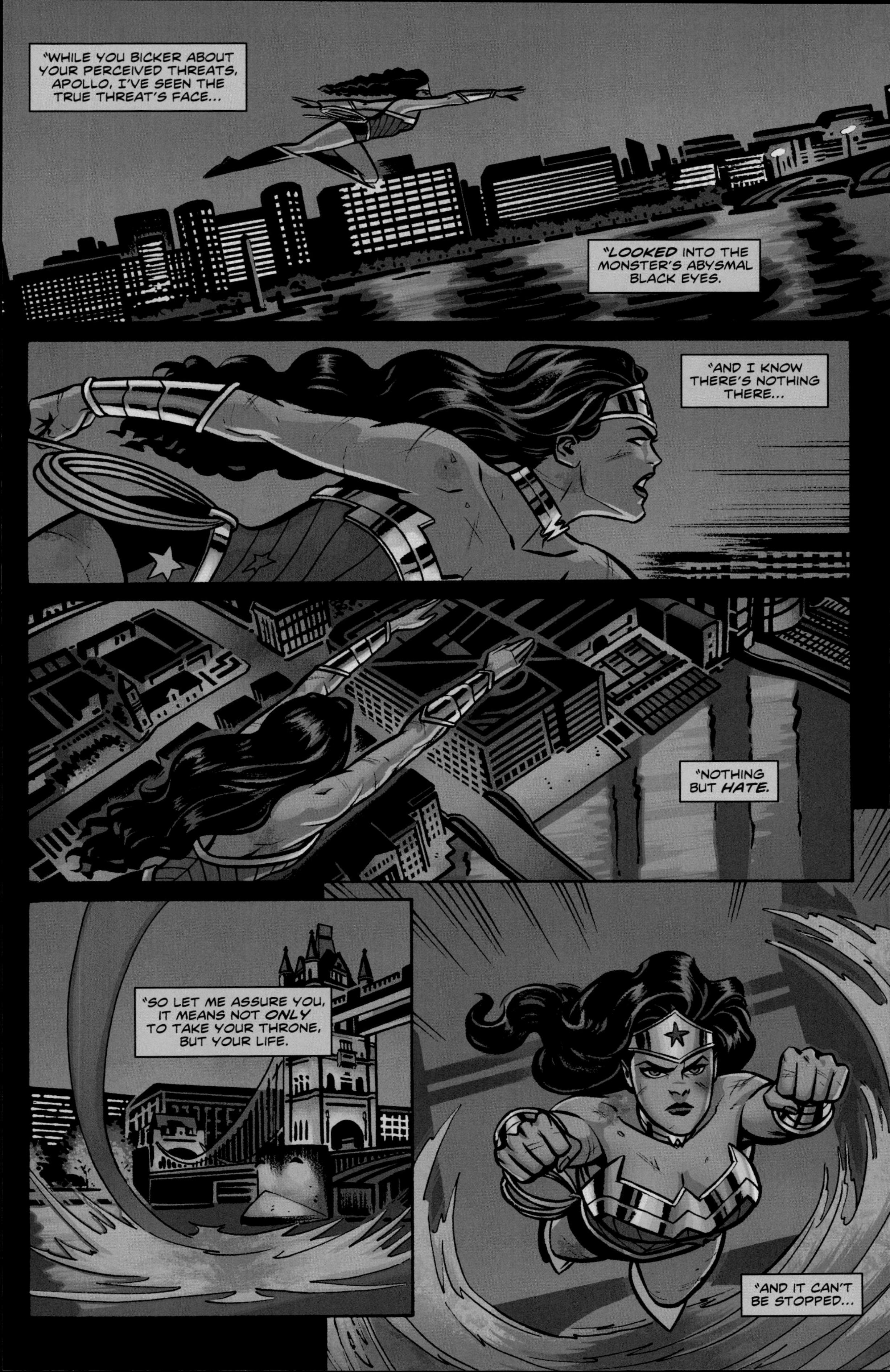
"WHILE YOU BICKER ABOUT YOUR PERCEIVED THREATS, APOLLO, I'VE SEEN THE TRUE THREAT'S FACE...
"LOOKED INTO THE MONSTER'S ABYSMAL BLACK EYES.
"AND I KNOW THERE'S NOTHING THERE...
"NOTHING BUT HATE.
"SO LET ME ASSURE YOU, IT MEANS NOT ONLY TO TAKE YOUR THRONE, BUT YOUR LIFE.
"AND IT CAN'T BE STOPPED...

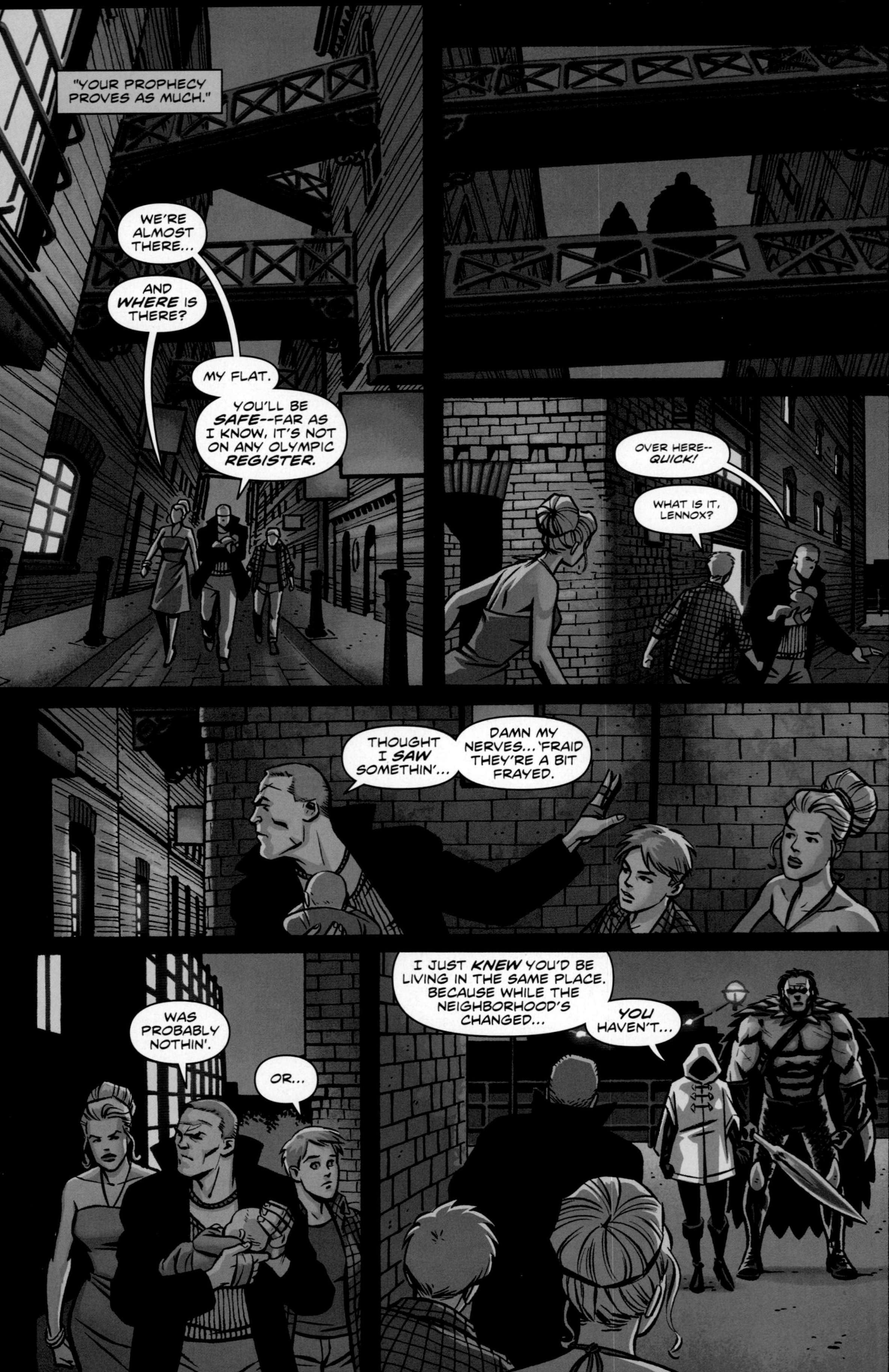
"YOUR PROPHECY PROVES AS MUCH."
WE'RE ALMOST THERE...
AND WHERE IS THERE?
MY FLAT.
YOU'LL BE SAFE--FAR AS I KNOW, IT'S NOT ON ANY OLYMPIC REGISTER.
OVER HERE--QUICK!
WHAT IS IT, LENNOX?
THOUGHT I SAW SOMETHIN'...
DAMN MY NERVES...'FRAID THEY'RE A BIT FRAYED.
WAS PROBABLY NOTHIN'.
OR...
I JUST KNEW YOU'D BE LIVING IN THE SAME PLACE. BECAUSE WHILE THE NEIGHBORHOOD'S CHANGED...
YOU HAVEN'T...

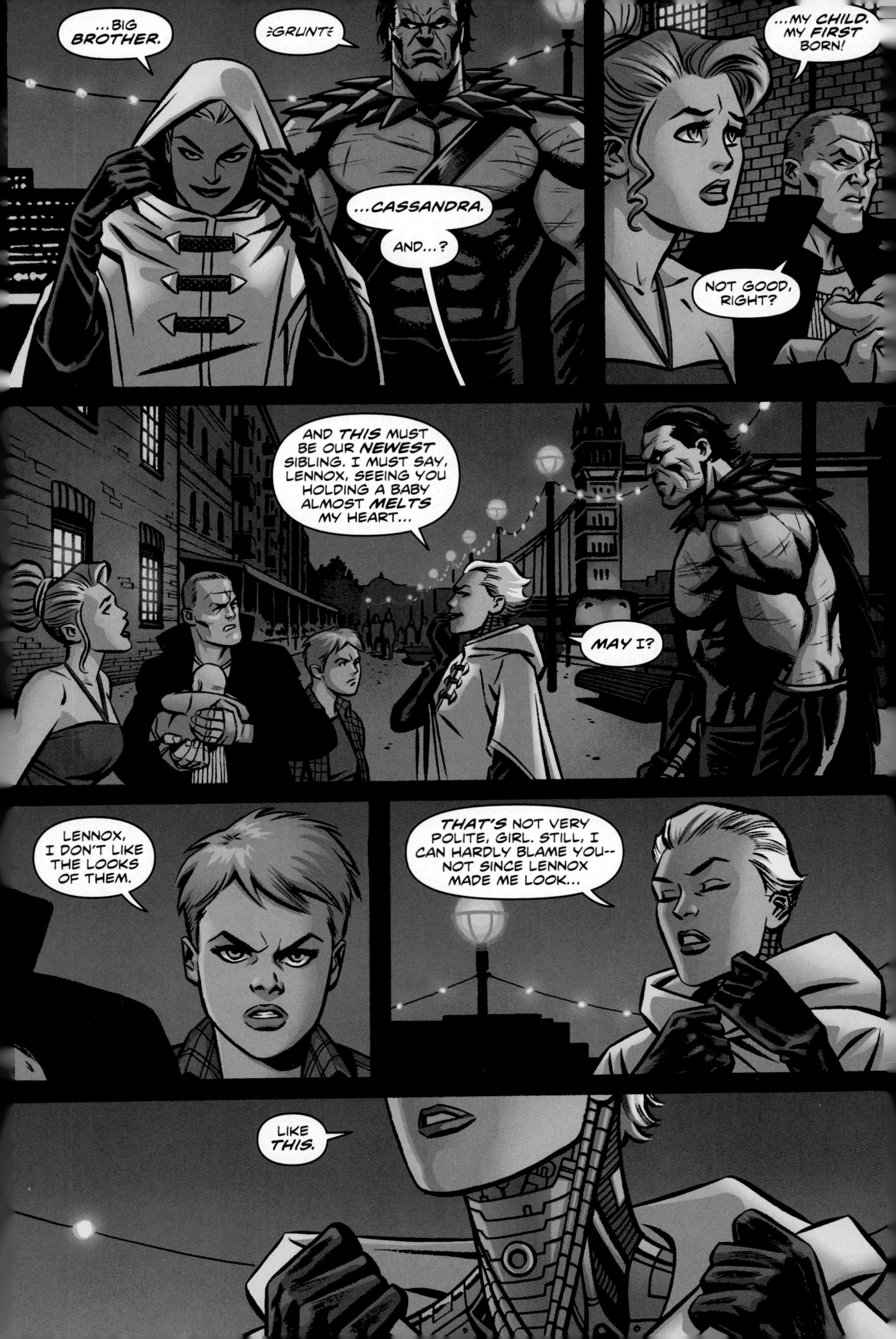
...BIG BROTHER.
GRUNT
...CASSANDRA.
AND...?
...MY CHILD. MY FIRST BORN!
NOT GOOD, RIGHT?
AND THIS MUST BE OUR NEWEST SIBLING. I MUST SAY, LENNOX, SEEING YOU HOLDING A BABY ALMOST MELTS MY HEART...
MAY I?
LENNOX, I DON'T LIKE THE LOOKS OF THEM.
THAT'S NOT VERY POLITE, GIRL. STILL, I CAN HARDLY BLAME YOU-- NOT SINCE LENNOX MADE ME LOOK...
LIKE THIS.

"IT'S TRUE, DEAR. THIRTY YEARS AGO, YOUR *KNIGHT* IN STONY ARMOR TORE OUT MY THROAT WITH HIS BARE *HANDS.*

"FOR *NO GOOD REASON.*"

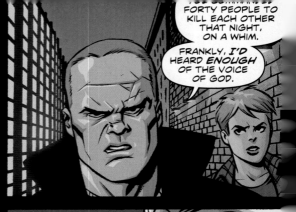

...FORTY PEOPLE TO KILL EACH OTHER THAT NIGHT, ON A WHIM.

FRANKLY, *I'D* HEARD *ENOUGH* OF THE VOICE OF GOD.

SO YOU TOOK IT UPON YOURSELF TO *SILENCE* IT?

AND YOU CALL *ME* CORRUPTED.

ENOUGH WITH THE WORDS...

I AGREE...

'CUZ I BEEN *DYIN'* TO HIT SOMETHIN' ALL *NIGHT...*

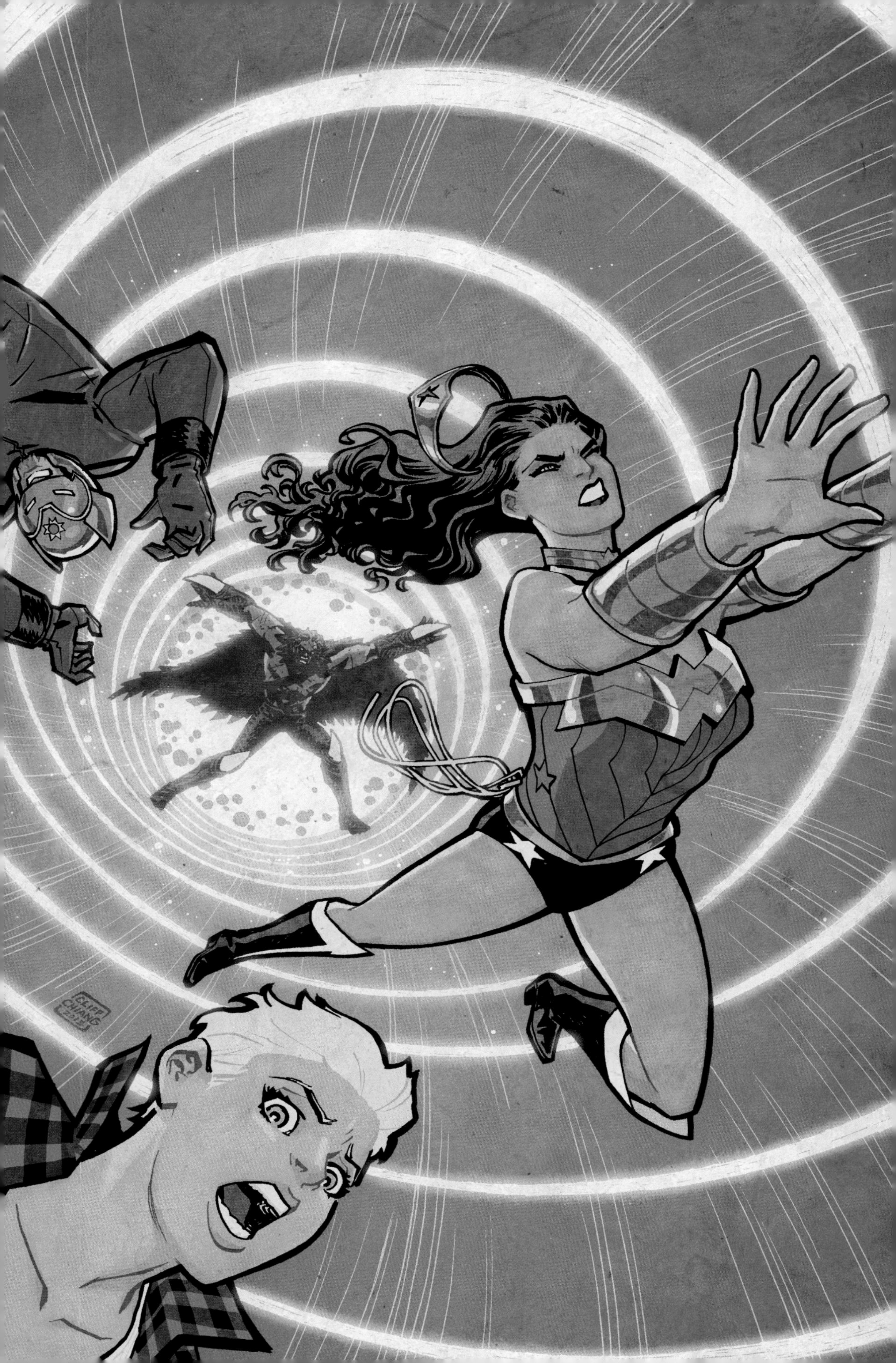
CLIFF
CHIANG
2013

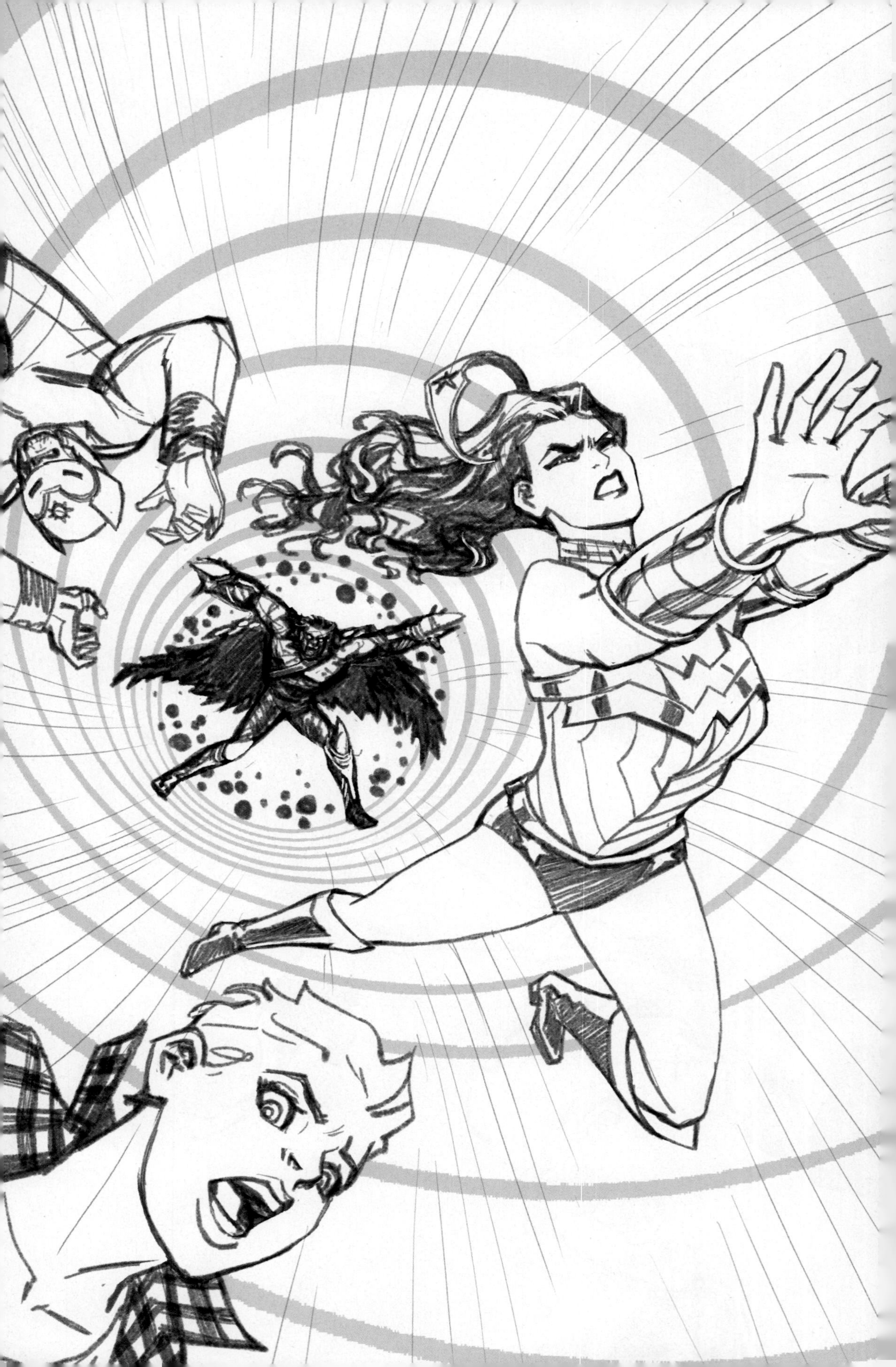

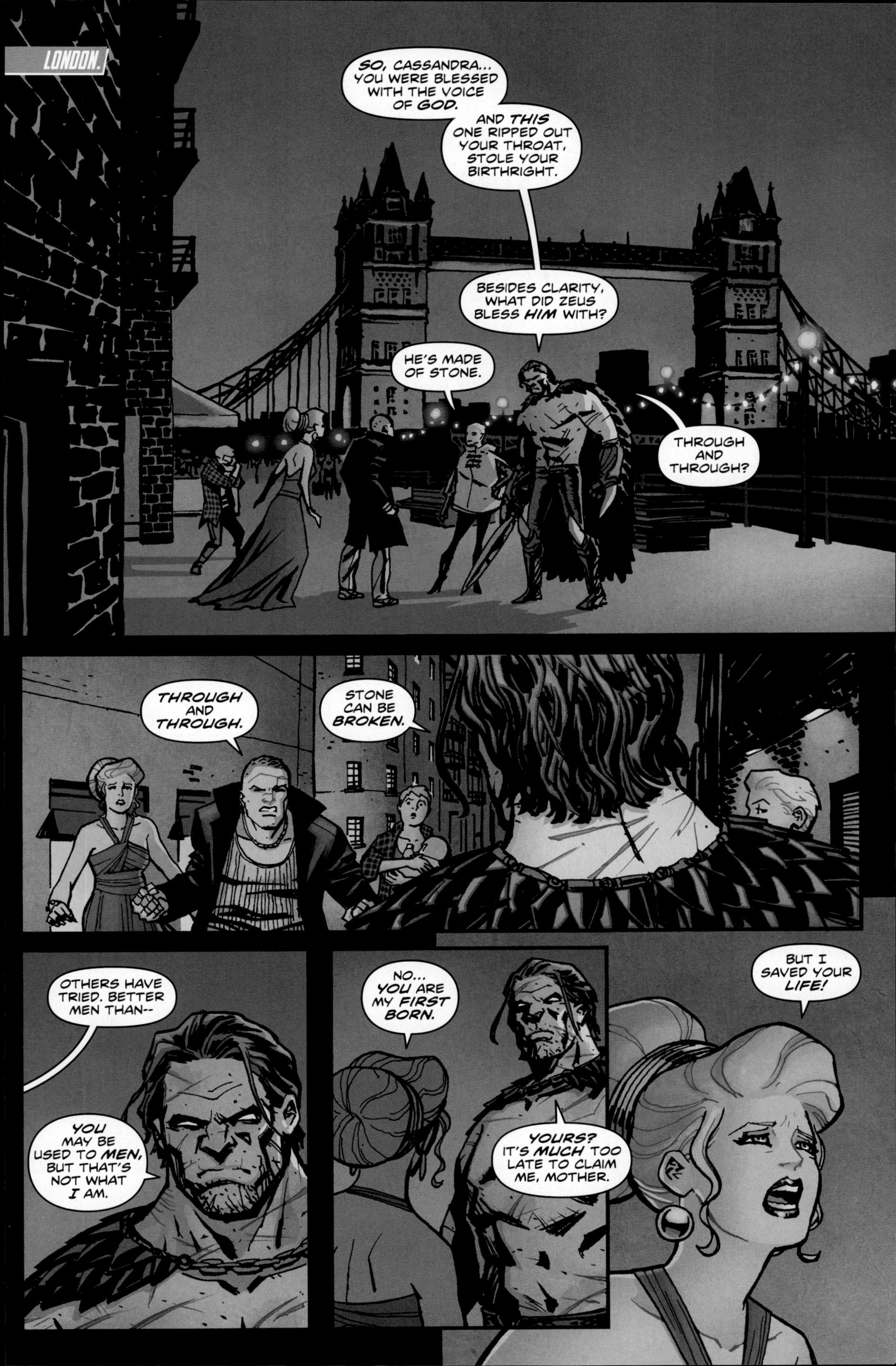
LONDON.
SO, CASSANDRA... YOU WERE BLESSED WITH THE VOICE OF GOD.
AND THIS ONE RIPPED OUT YOUR THROAT, STOLE YOUR BIRTHRIGHT.
BESIDES CLARITY, WHAT DID ZEUS BLESS HIM WITH?
HE'S MADE OF STONE.
THROUGH AND THROUGH?
THROUGH AND THROUGH.
STONE CAN BE BROKEN.
OTHERS HAVE TRIED. BETTER MEN THAN--
YOU MAY BE USED TO MEN, BUT THAT'S NOT WHAT I AM.
NO... YOU ARE MY FIRST BORN.
YOURS? IT'S MUCH TOO LATE TO CLAIM ME, MOTHER.
BUT I SAVED YOUR LIFE!

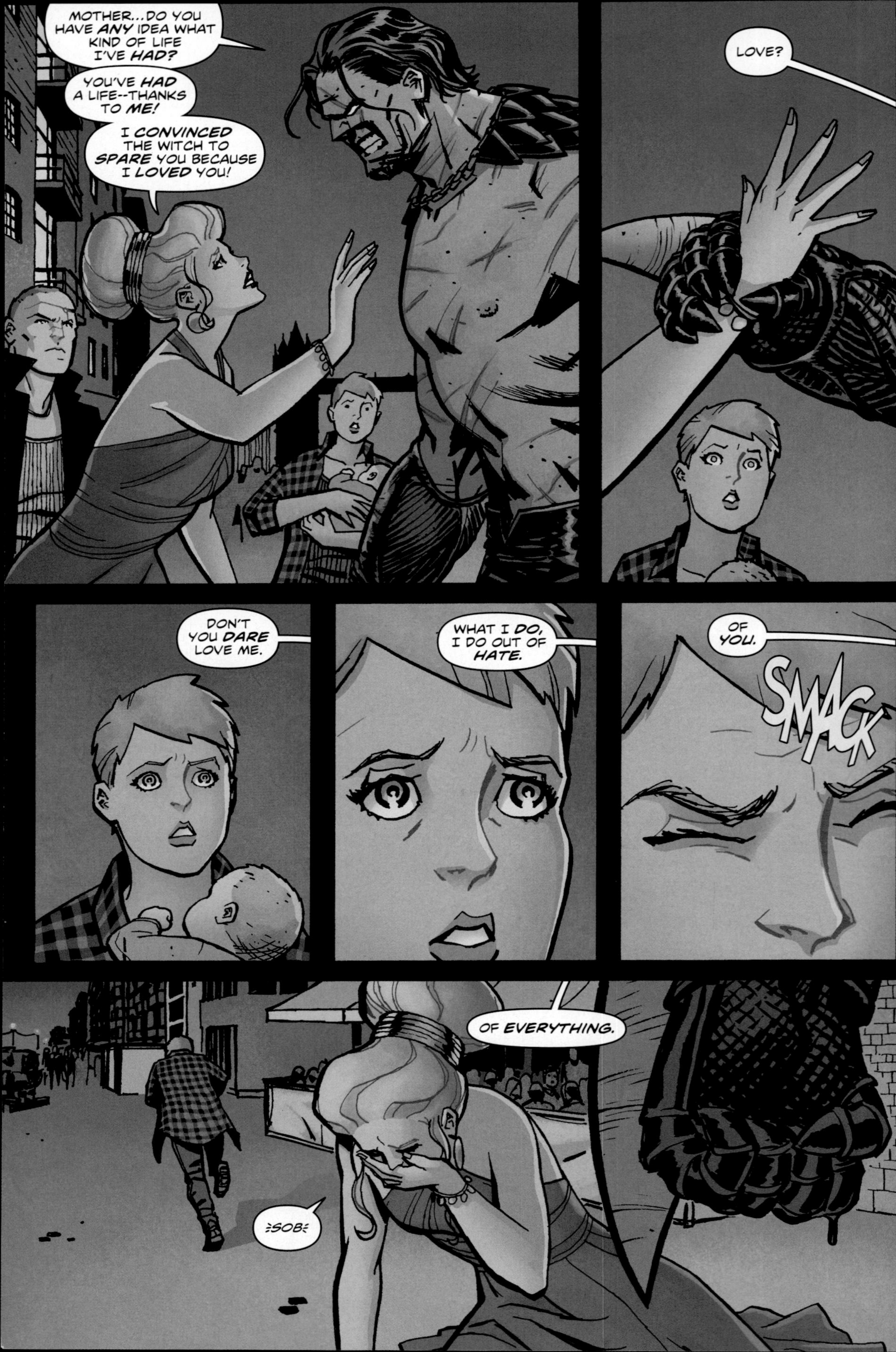
MOTHER...DO YOU HAVE ANY IDEA WHAT KIND OF LIFE I'VE HAD?
YOU'VE HAD A LIFE--THANKS TO ME!
I CONVINCED THE WITCH TO SPARE YOU BECAUSE I LOVED YOU!
LOVE?
DON'T YOU DARE LOVE ME.
WHAT I DO, I DO OUT OF HATE.
OF YOU.
SMACK
OF EVERYTHING.
SOB

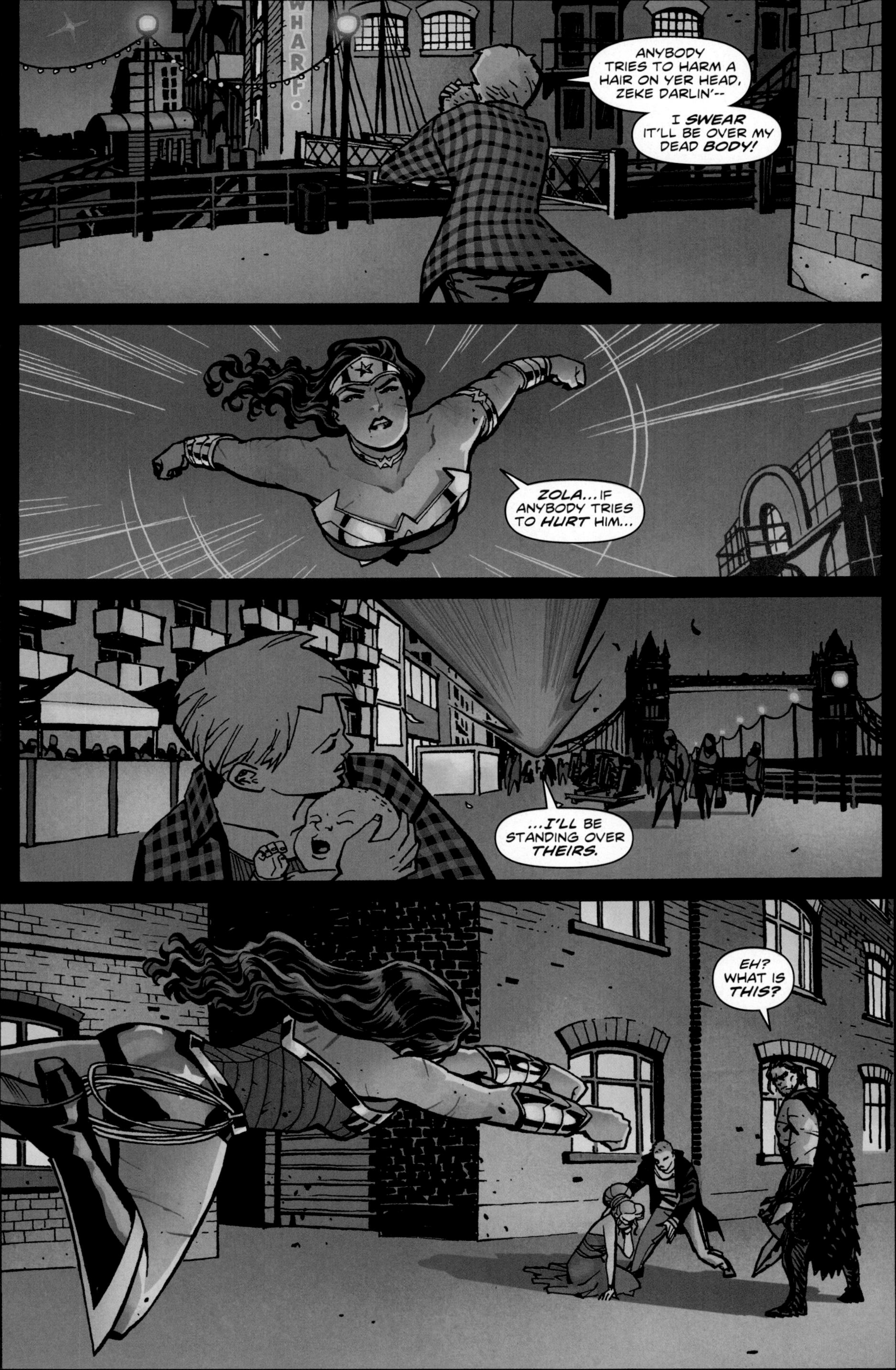

WHARF.
ANYBODY TRIES TO HARM A HAIR ON YER HEAD, ZEKE DARLIN'--
I SWEAR IT'LL BE OVER MY DEAD BODY!
ZOLA... IF ANYBODY TRIES TO HURT HIM...
...I'LL BE STANDING OVER THEIRS.
EH? WHAT IS THIS?

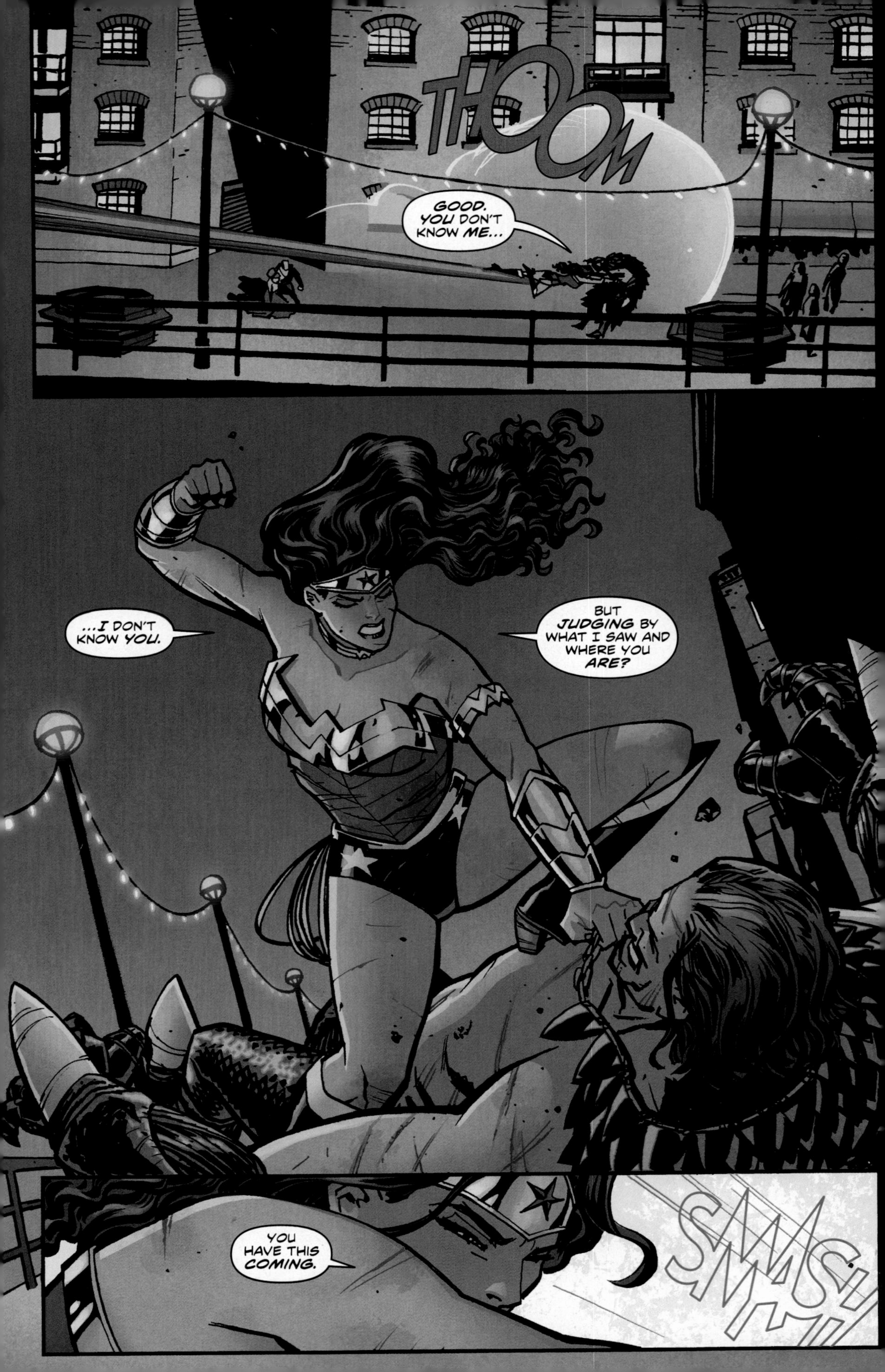
THOOM
GOOD. YOU DON'T KNOW ME...
...I DON'T KNOW YOU.
BUT JUDGING BY WHAT I SAW AND WHERE YOU ARE?
YOU HAVE THIS COMING.
SMASH

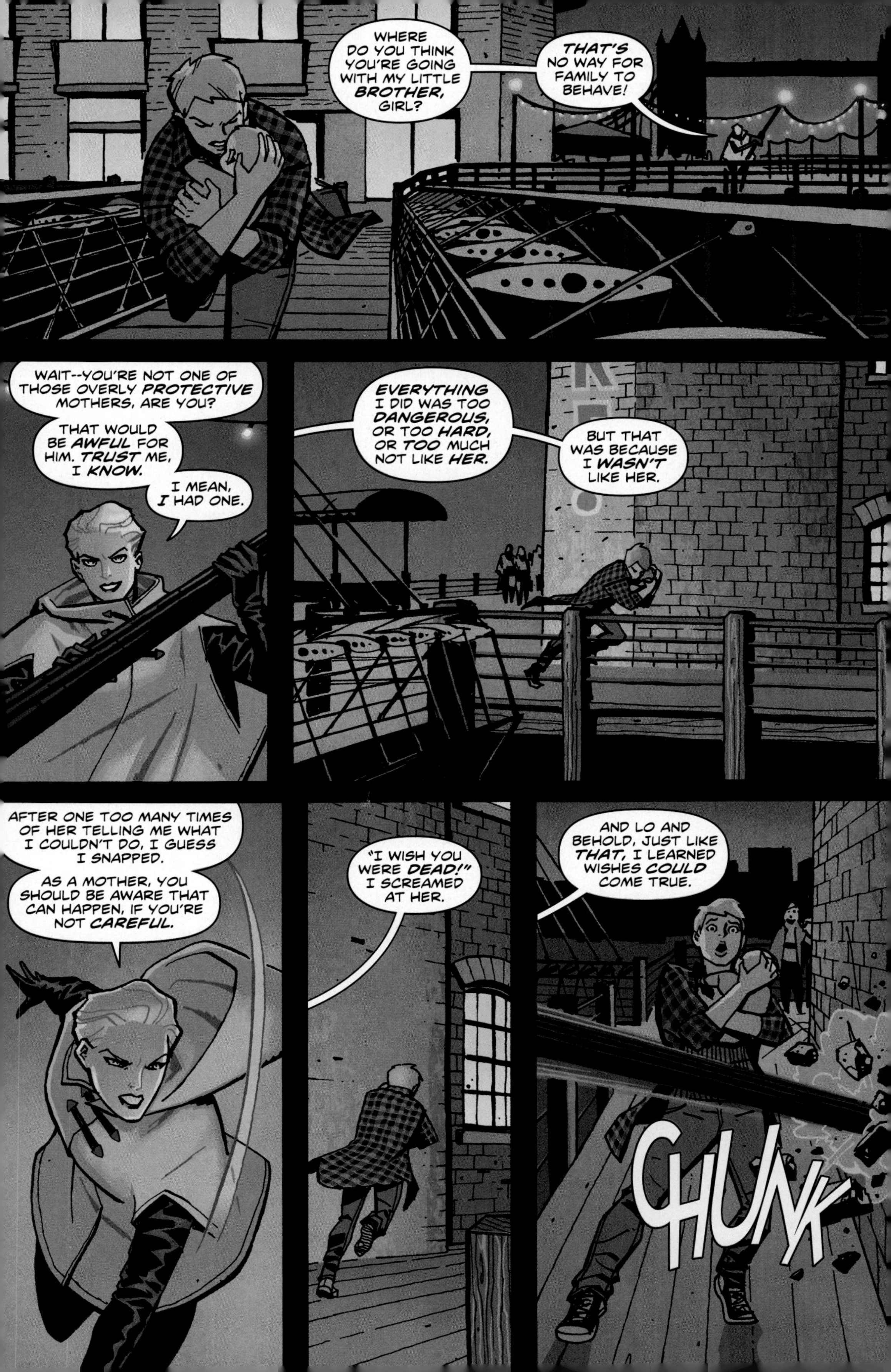
WHERE DO YOU THINK YOU'RE GOING WITH MY LITTLE BROTHER, GIRL?
THAT'S NO WAY FOR FAMILY TO BEHAVE!
WAIT--YOU'RE NOT ONE OF THOSE OVERLY PROTECTIVE MOTHERS, ARE YOU?
THAT WOULD BE AWFUL FOR HIM. TRUST ME, I KNOW.
I MEAN, I HAD ONE.
EVERYTHING I DID WAS TOO DANGEROUS, OR TOO HARD, OR TOO MUCH NOT LIKE HER.
BUT THAT WAS BECAUSE I WASN'T LIKE HER.
AFTER ONE TOO MANY TIMES OF HER TELLING ME WHAT I COULDN'T DO, I GUESS I SNAPPED.
AS A MOTHER, YOU SHOULD BE AWARE THAT CAN HAPPEN, IF YOU'RE NOT CAREFUL.
"I WISH YOU WERE DEAD!" I SCREAMED AT HER.
AND LO AND BEHOLD, JUST LIKE THAT, I LEARNED WISHES COULD COME TRUE.
CHUNK

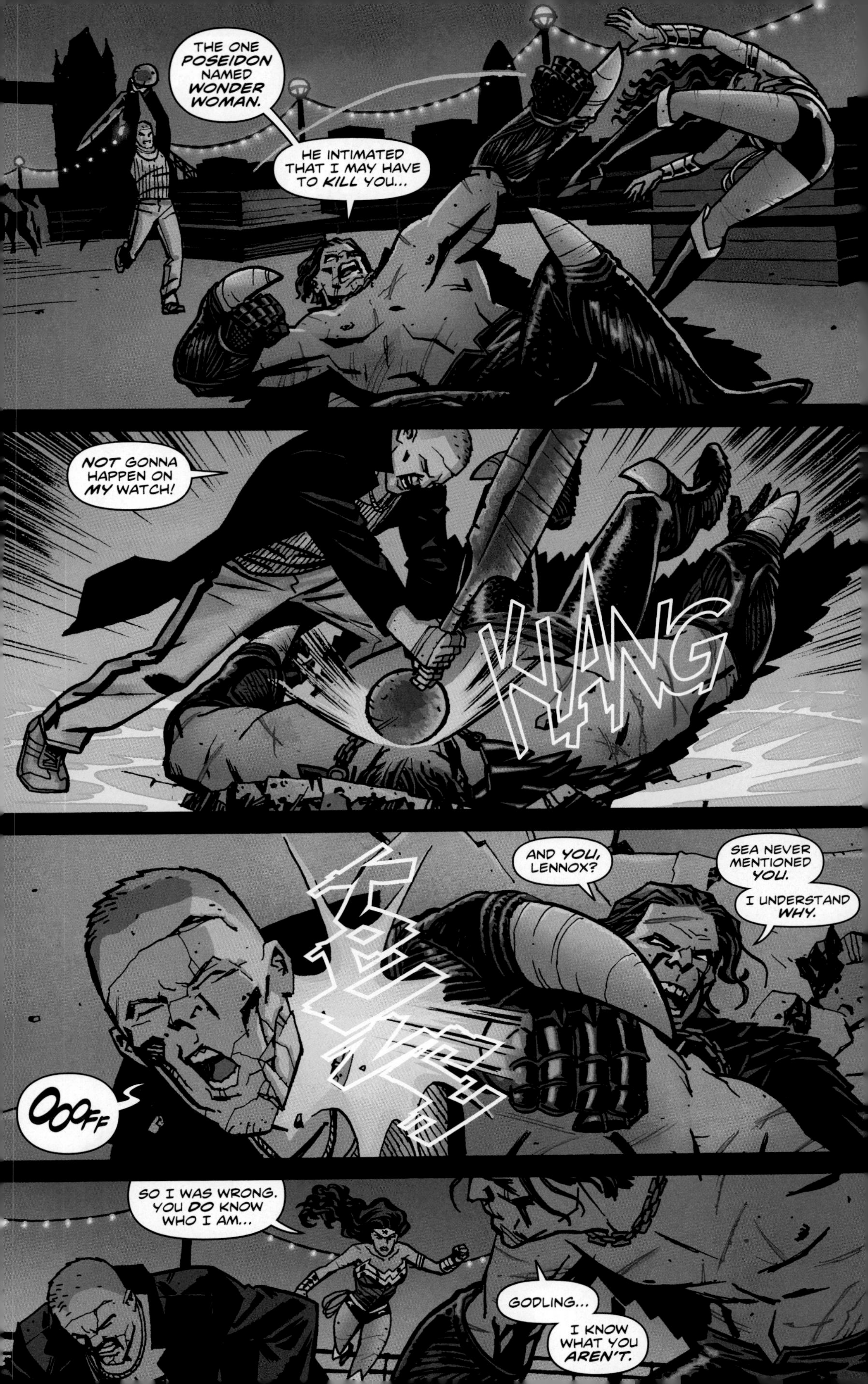
THE ONE POSEIDON NAMED WONDER WOMAN.
HE INTIMATED THAT I MAY HAVE TO KILL YOU...
NOT GONNA HAPPEN ON MY WATCH!
AND YOU, LENNOX?
SEA NEVER MENTIONED YOU.
I UNDERSTAND WHY.
OOOFF
SO I WAS WRONG. YOU DO KNOW WHO I AM...
GODLING...
I KNOW WHAT YOU AREN'T.

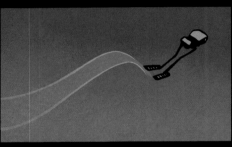

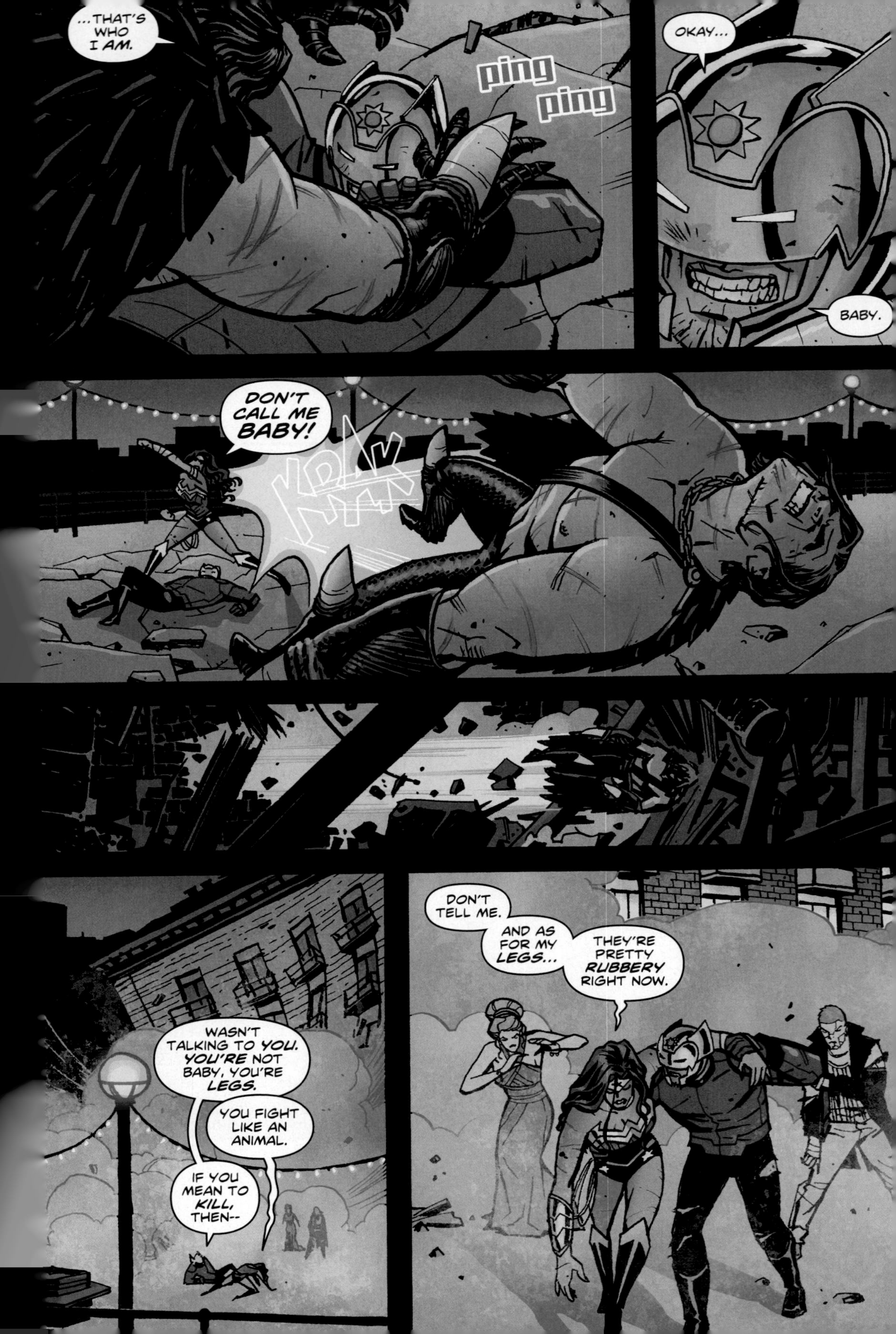
...THAT'S WHO I AM.
ping ping
OKAY...
BABY.
DON'T CALL ME BABY!
KRAK
DON'T TELL ME.
AND AS FOR MY LEGS...
THEY'RE PRETTY RUBBERY RIGHT NOW.
WASN'T TALKING TO YOU. YOU'RE NOT BABY, YOU'RE LEGS.
YOU FIGHT LIKE AN ANIMAL.
IF YOU MEAN TO KILL, THEN--

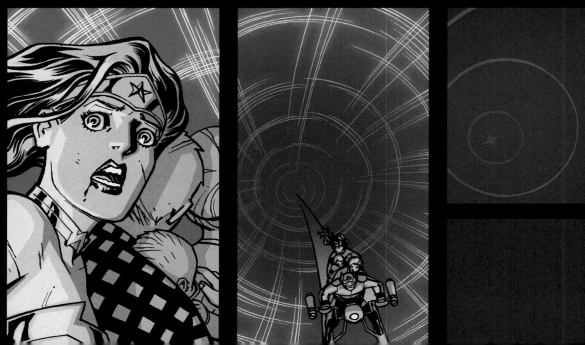

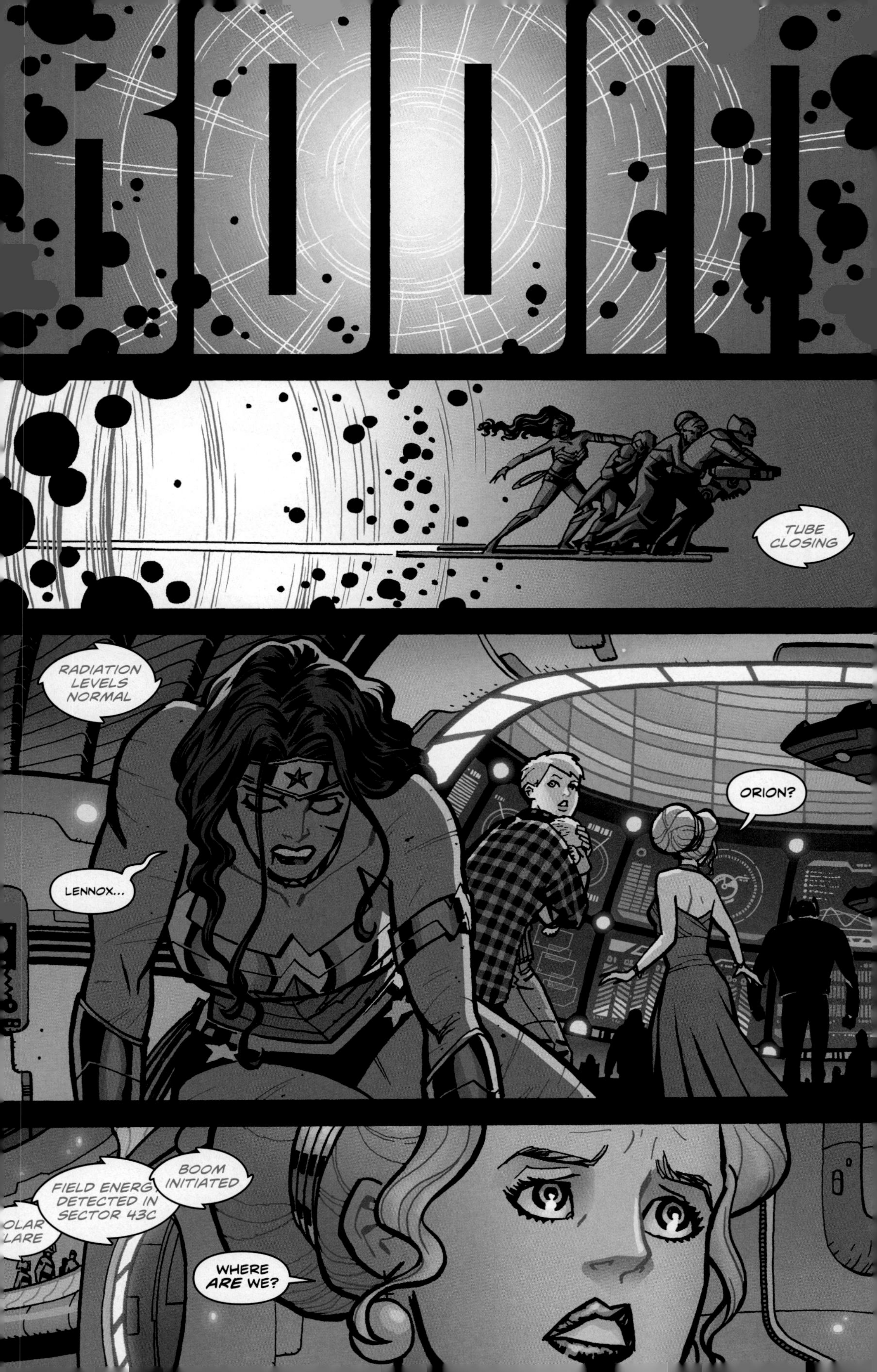
TUBE CLOSING
RADIATION LEVELS NORMAL
ORION?
LENNOX...
BOOM INITIATED
FIELD ENERG DETECTED IN SECTOR 43C
OLAR LARE
WHERE ARE WE?

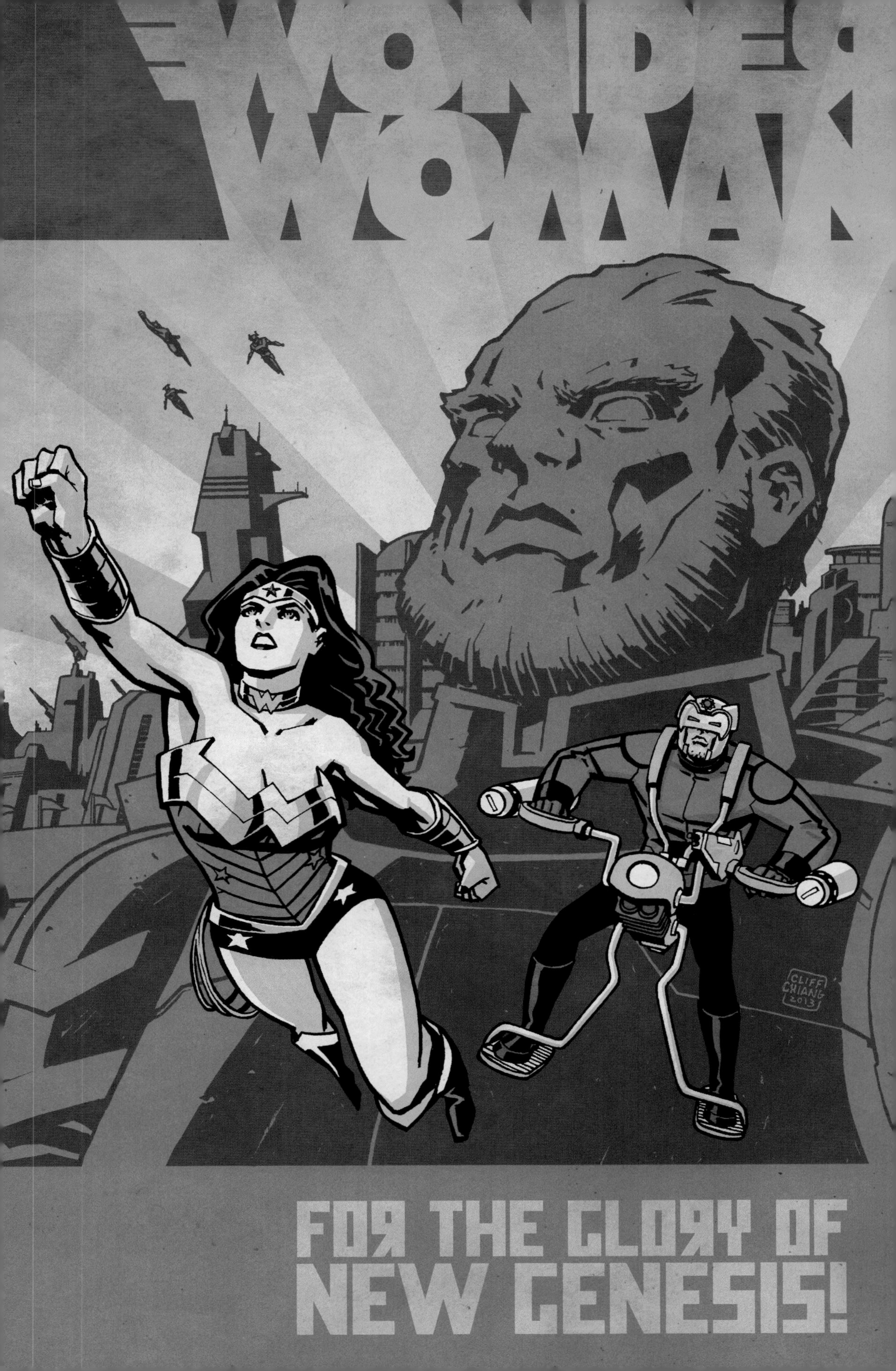
WONDER WOMAN
CLIFF CHIANG 2013
FOR THE GLORY OF
NEW GENESIS!

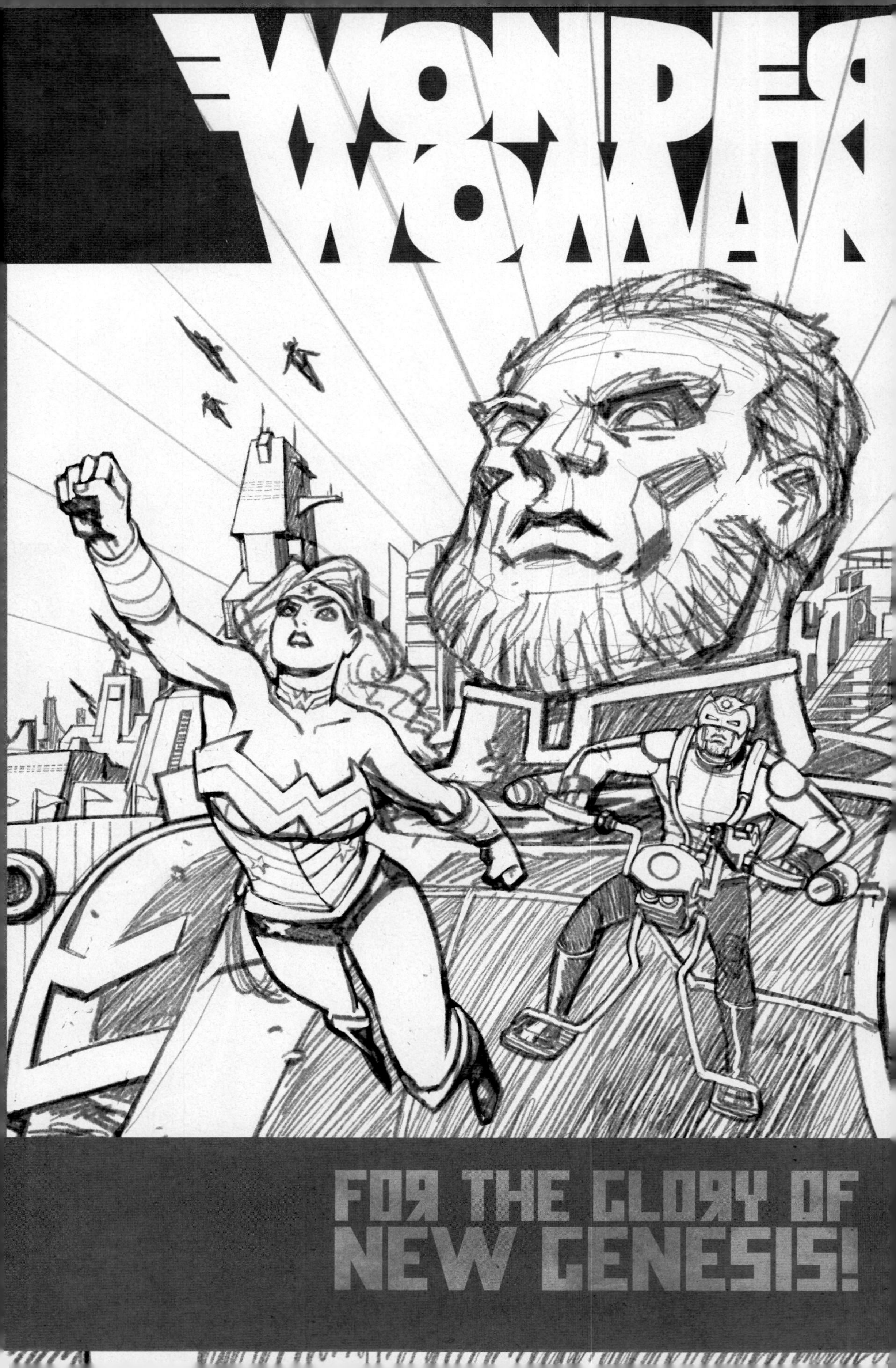
WONDER WOMAN
FOR THE GLORY OF
NEW GENESIS!

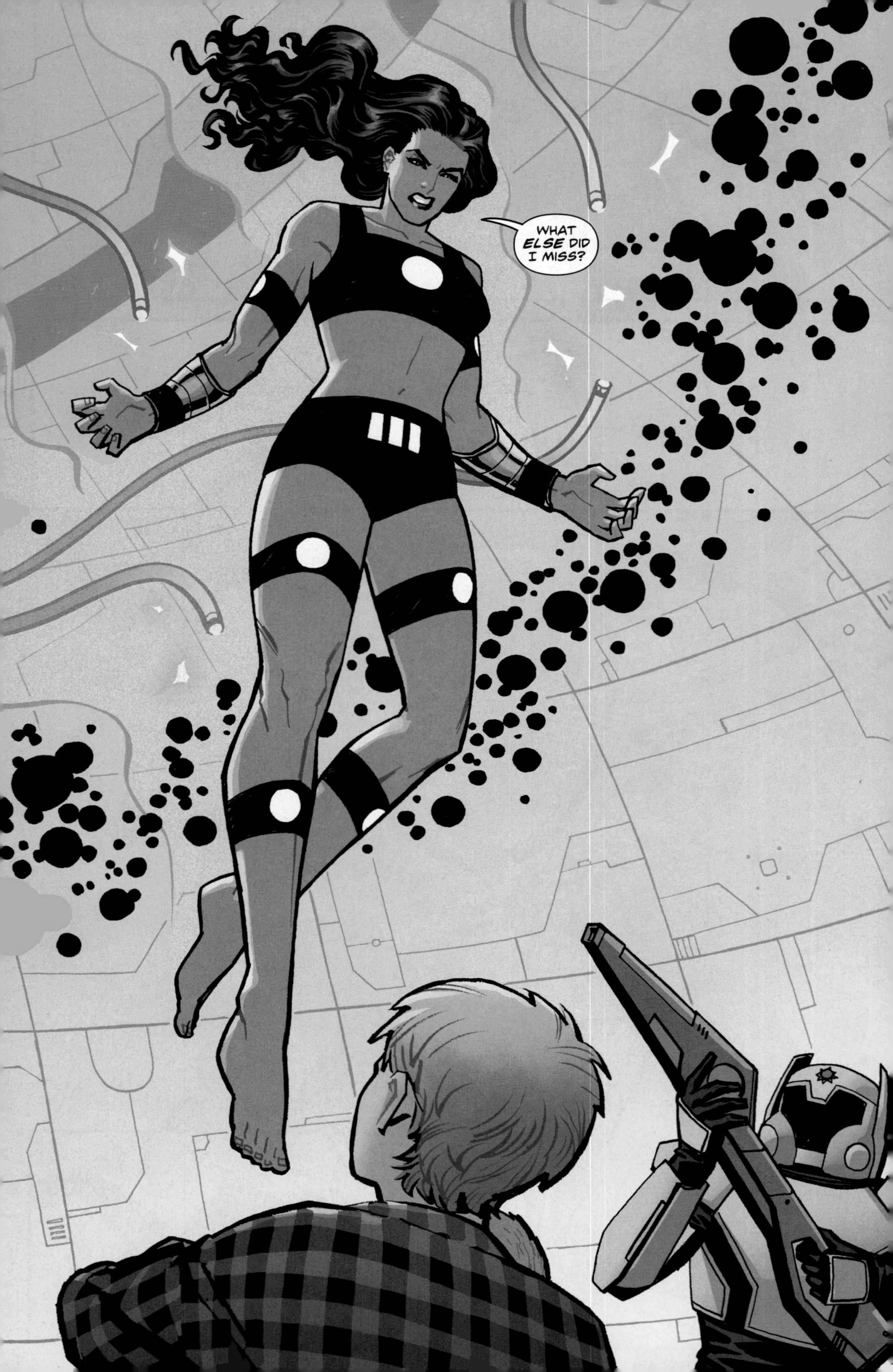
WHAT *ELSE* DID I MISS?

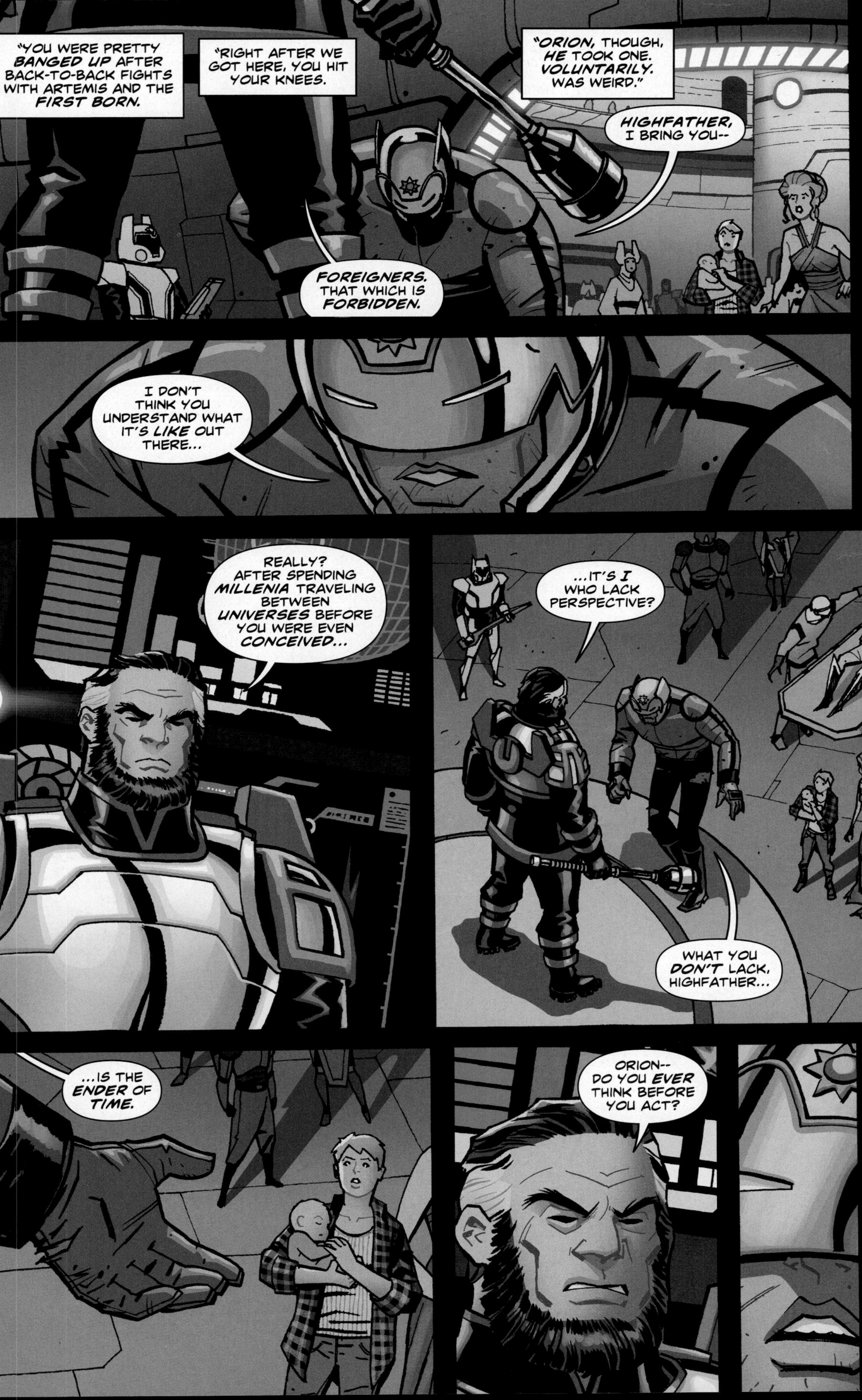
"YOU WERE PRETTY BANGED UP AFTER BACK-TO-BACK FIGHTS WITH ARTEMIS AND THE FIRST BORN.
"RIGHT AFTER WE GOT HERE, YOU HIT YOUR KNEES.
"ORION, THOUGH, HE TOOK ONE. VOLUNTARILY. WAS WEIRD."
HIGHFATHER, I BRING YOU--
FOREIGNERS. THAT WHICH IS FORBIDDEN.
I DON'T THINK YOU UNDERSTAND WHAT IT'S LIKE OUT THERE...
REALLY? AFTER SPENDING MILLENIA TRAVELING BETWEEN UNIVERSES BEFORE YOU WERE EVEN CONCEIVED...
...IT'S I WHO LACK PERSPECTIVE?
WHAT YOU DON'T LACK, HIGHFATHER...
...IS THE ENDER OF TIME.
ORION-- DO YOU EVER THINK BEFORE YOU ACT?

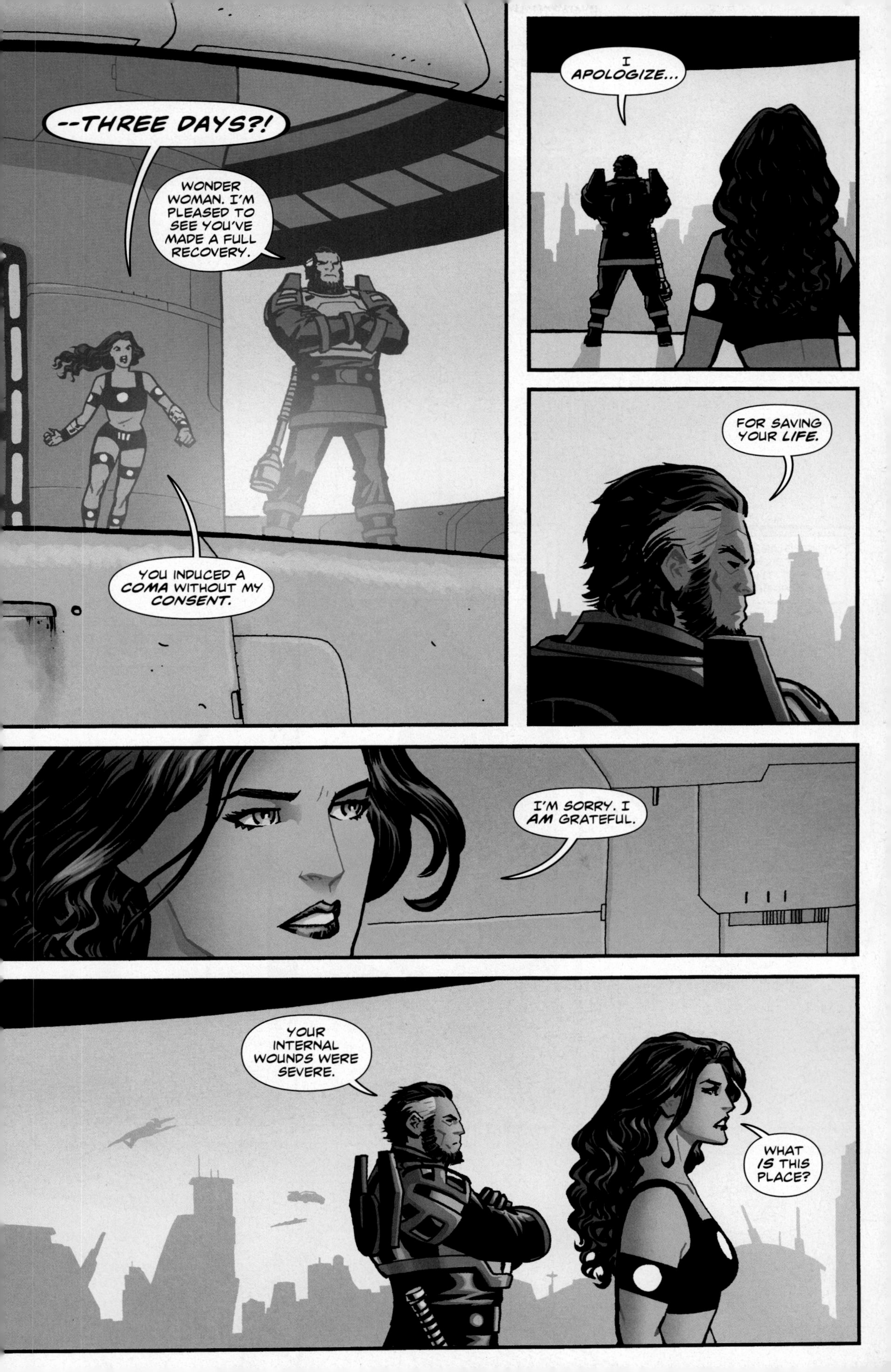
--THREE DAYS?!
WONDER WOMAN. I'M PLEASED TO SEE YOU'VE MADE A FULL RECOVERY.
YOU INDUCED A COMA WITHOUT MY CONSENT.
I APOLOGIZE...
FOR SAVING YOUR LIFE.
I'M SORRY. I AM GRATEFUL.
YOUR INTERNAL WOUNDS WERE SEVERE.
WHAT IS THIS PLACE?

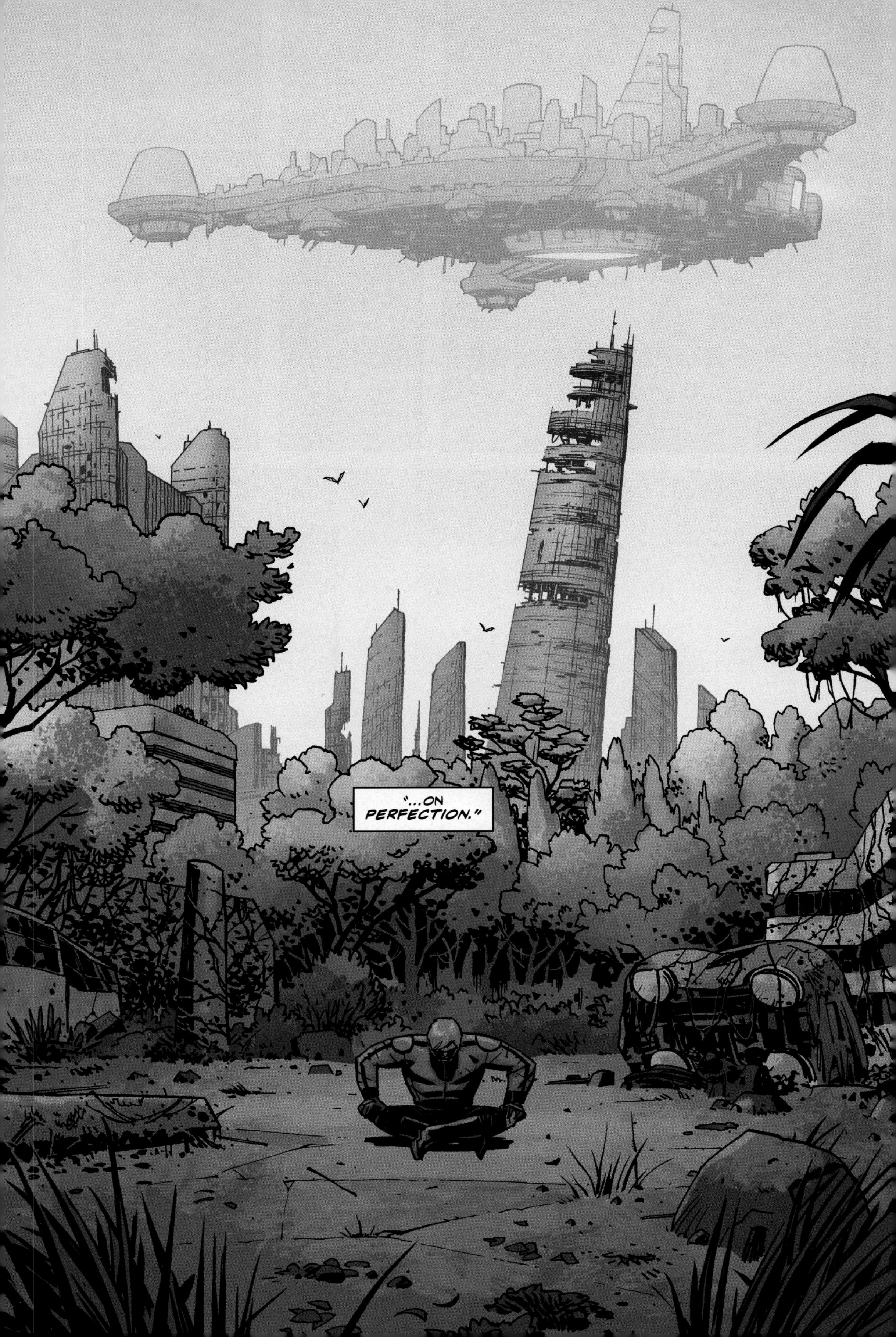
"...ON PERFECTION."

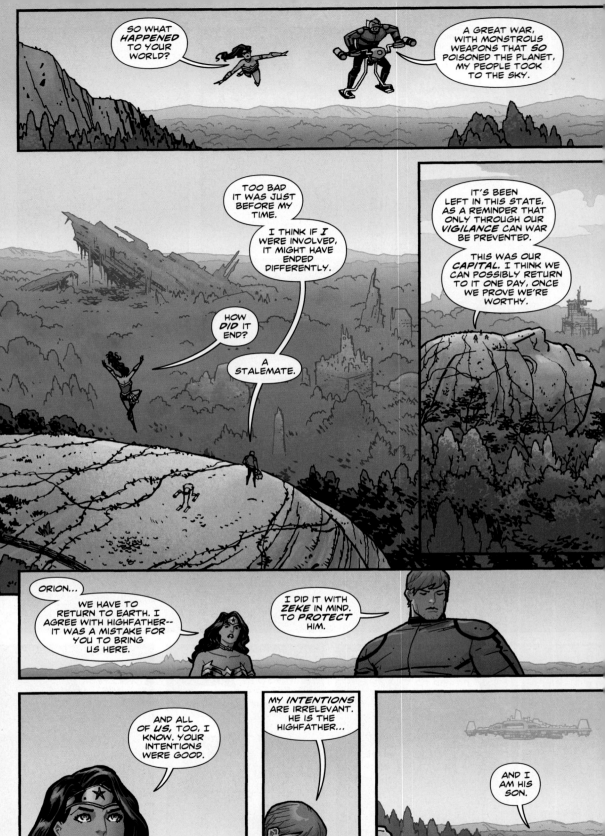

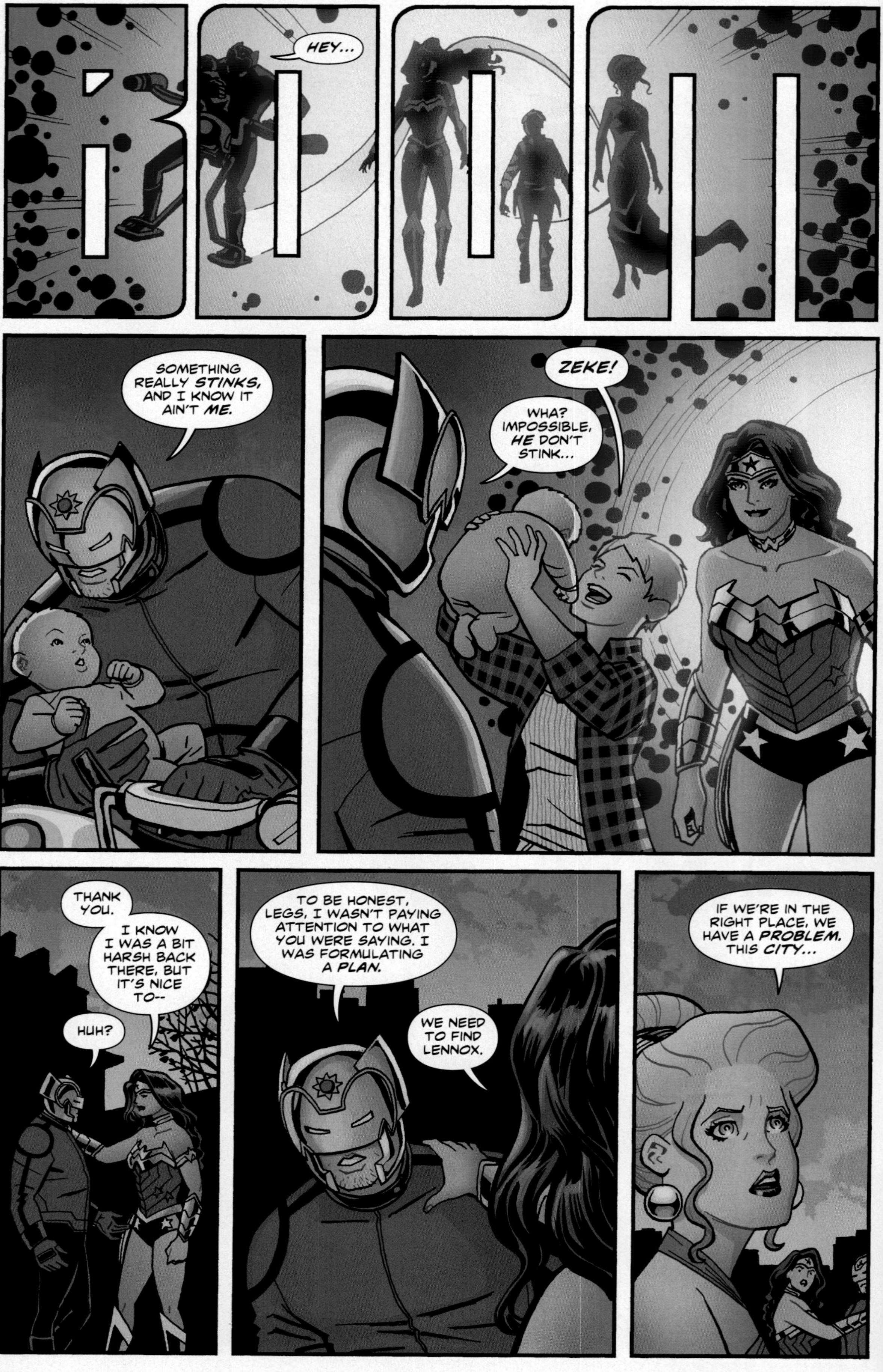
HEY...
SOMETHING REALLY STINKS, AND I KNOW IT AIN'T ME.
ZEKE!
WHA? IMPOSSIBLE, HE DON'T STINK...
THANK YOU.
I KNOW I WAS A BIT HARSH BACK THERE, BUT IT'S NICE TO--
HUH?
TO BE HONEST, LEGS, I WASN'T PAYING ATTENTION TO WHAT YOU WERE SAYING. I WAS FORMULATING A PLAN.
WE NEED TO FIND LENNOX.
IF WE'RE IN THE RIGHT PLACE, WE HAVE A PROBLEM. THIS CITY...

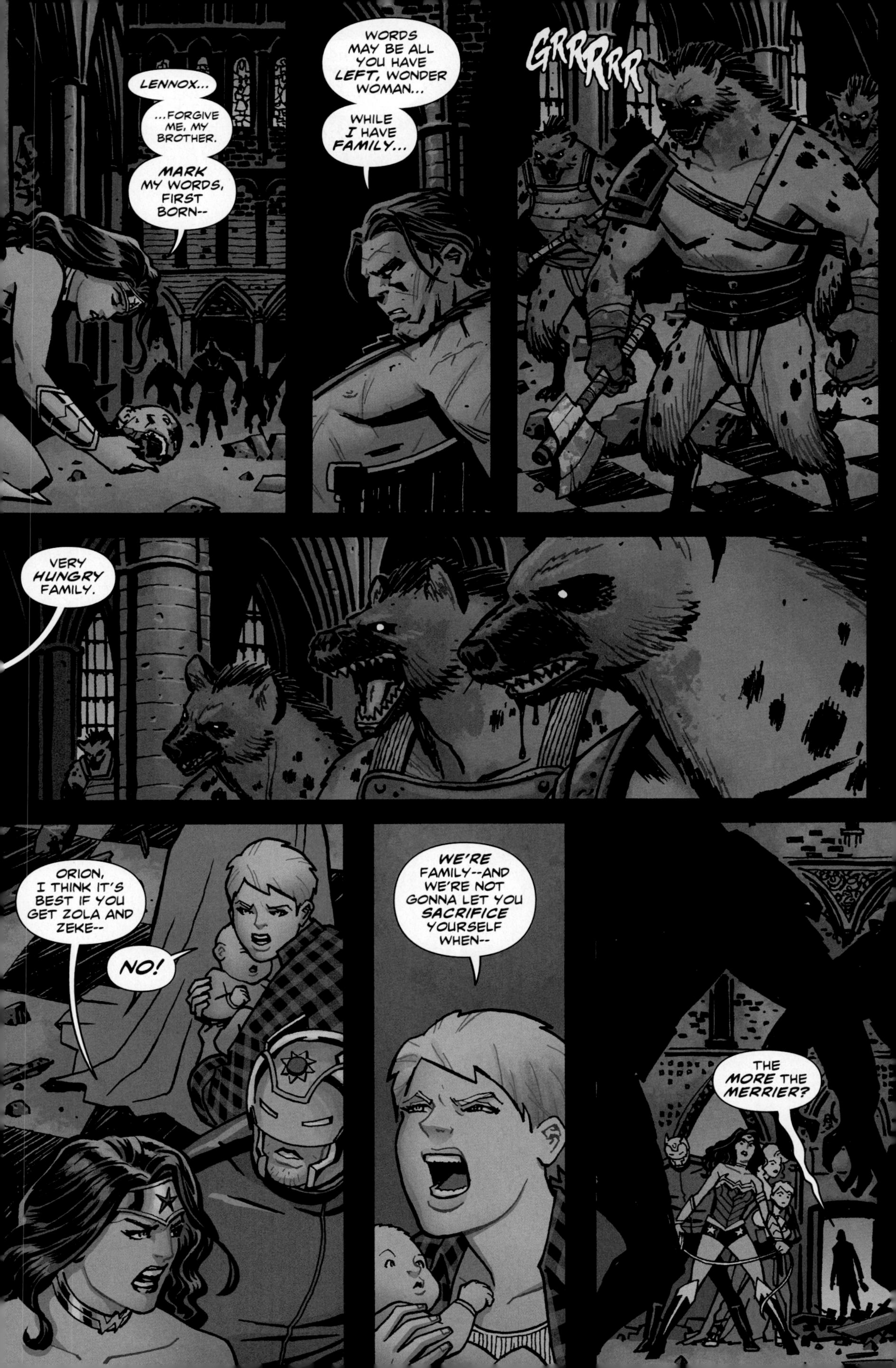

LENNOX...
...FORGIVE ME, MY BROTHER.
MARK MY WORDS, FIRST BORN--
WORDS MAY BE ALL YOU HAVE LEFT, WONDER WOMAN...
WHILE I HAVE FAMILY...
GRRRRRR
VERY HUNGRY FAMILY.
ORION, I THINK IT'S BEST IF YOU GET ZOLA AND ZEKE--
NO!
WE'RE FAMILY--AND WE'RE NOT GONNA LET YOU SACRIFICE YOURSELF WHEN--
THE MORE THE MERRIER?

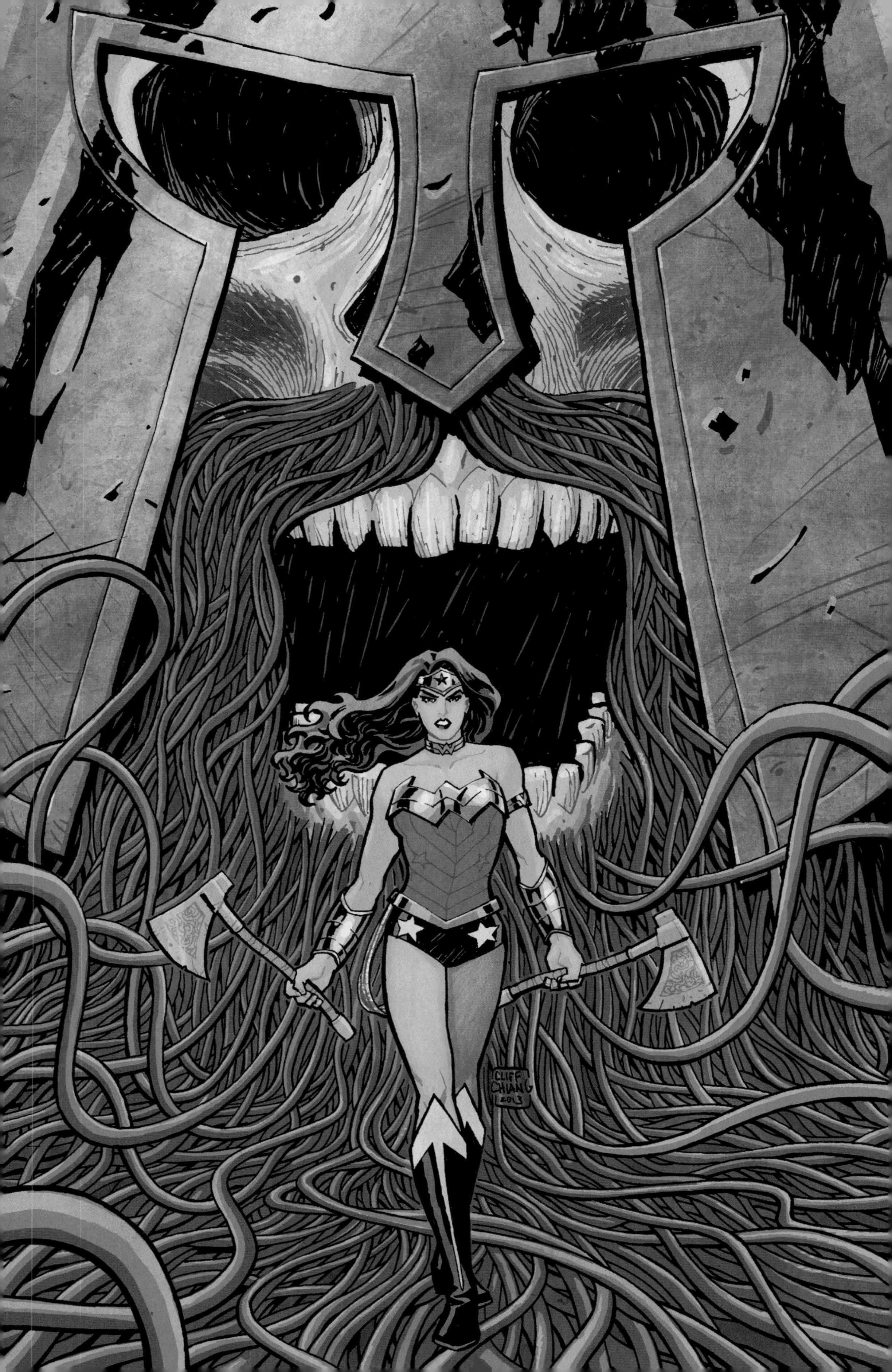
CLIFF CHIANG 2013

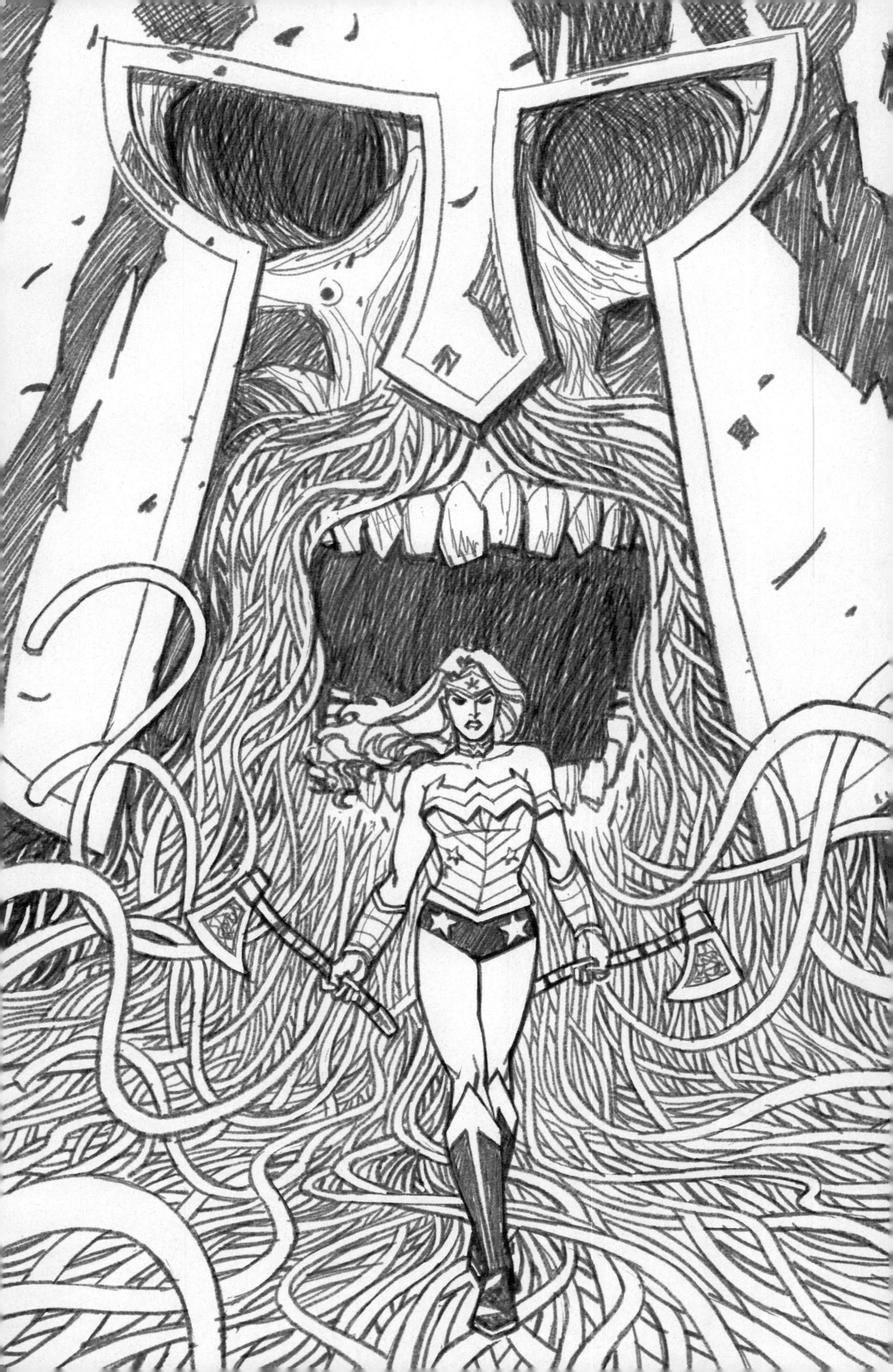

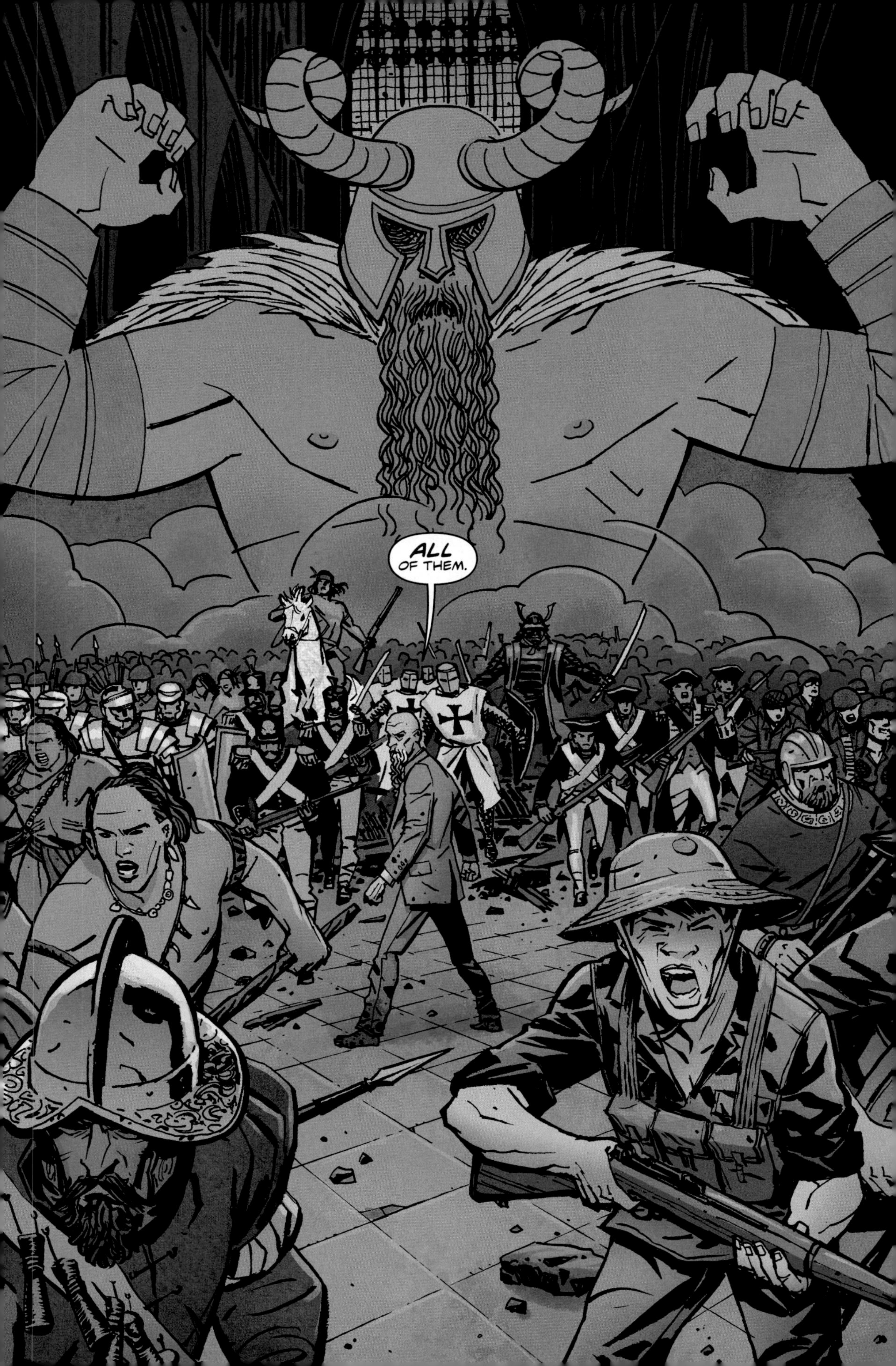
ALL OF THEM.

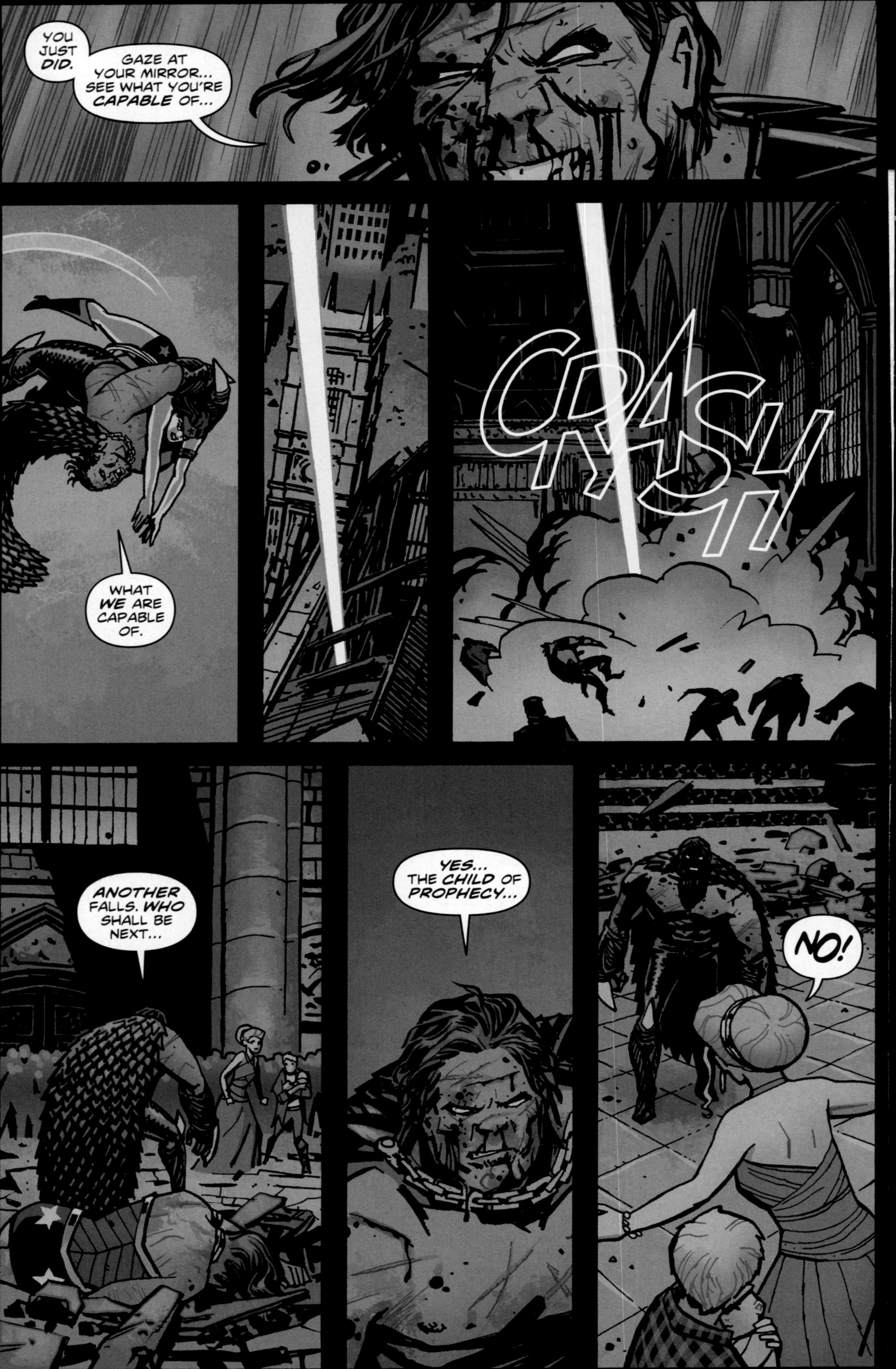

YOU JUST DID.
GAZE AT YOUR MIRROR... SEE WHAT YOU'RE CAPABLE OF...
WHAT WE ARE CAPABLE OF.
CRASH
ANOTHER FALLS. WHO SHALL BE NEXT...
YES... THE CHILD OF PROPHECY...
NO!

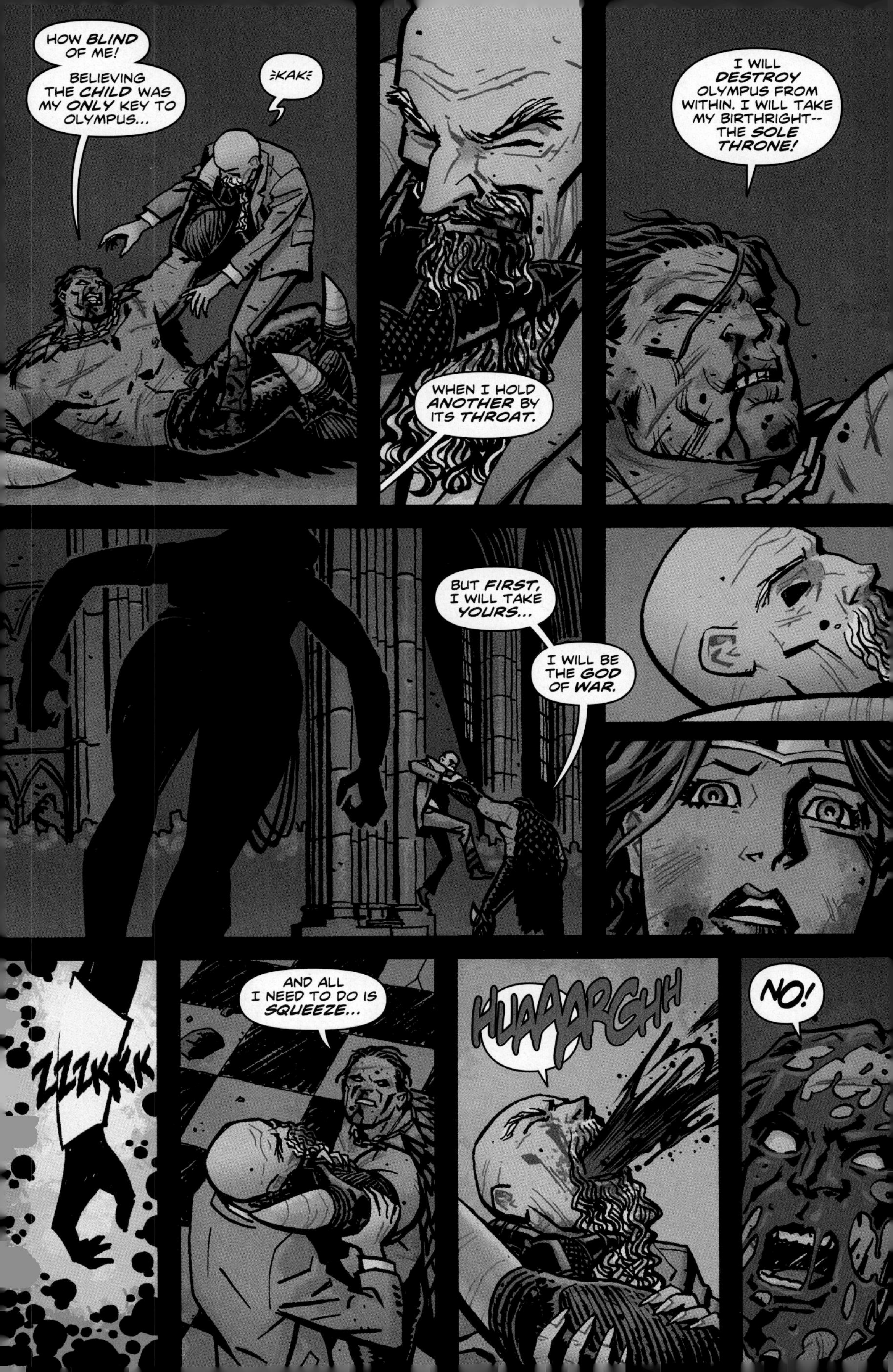
HOW BLIND OF ME!
BELIEVING THE CHILD WAS MY ONLY KEY TO OLYMPUS...
KAK
WHEN I HOLD ANOTHER BY ITS THROAT.
I WILL DESTROY OLYMPUS FROM WITHIN. I WILL TAKE MY BIRTHRIGHT-- THE SOLE THRONE!
BUT FIRST, I WILL TAKE YOURS...
I WILL BE THE GOD OF WAR.
ZZZKKKK
AND ALL I NEED TO DO IS SQUEEZE...
HUAAARGHH
NO!

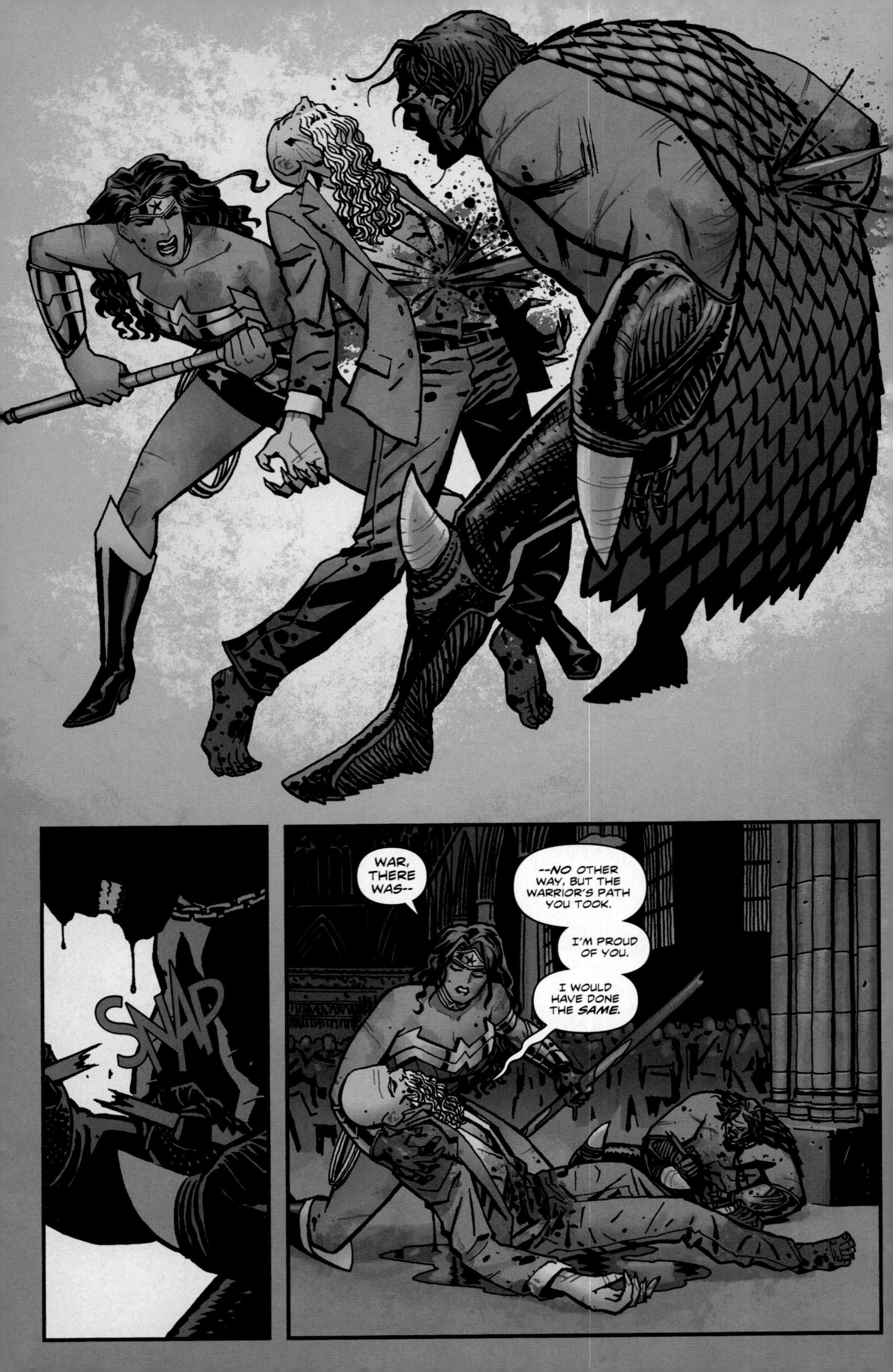
SNAP
WAR, THERE WAS--
--NO OTHER WAY, BUT THE WARRIOR'S PATH YOU TOOK.
I'M PROUD OF YOU.
I WOULD HAVE DONE THE SAME.

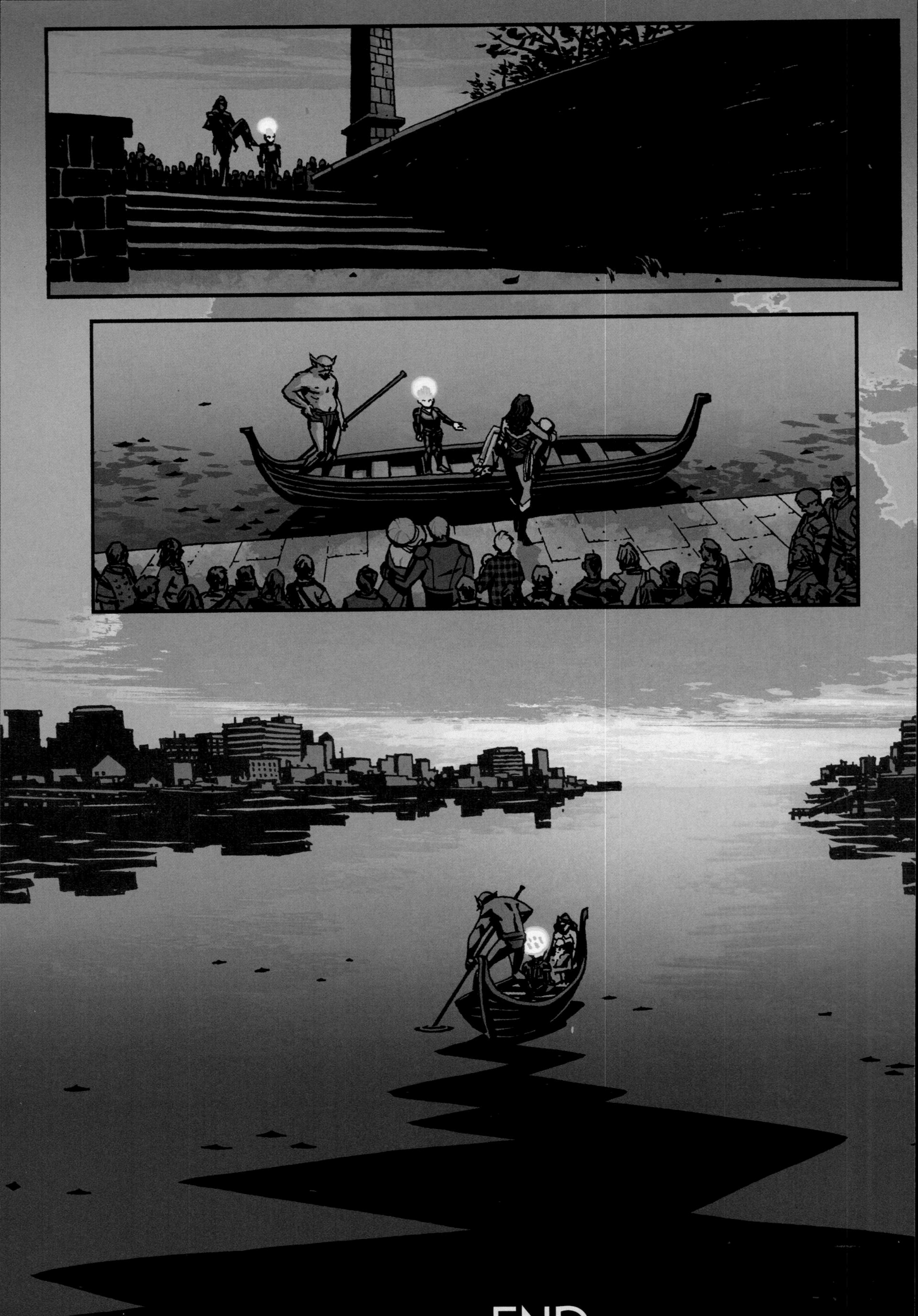
END

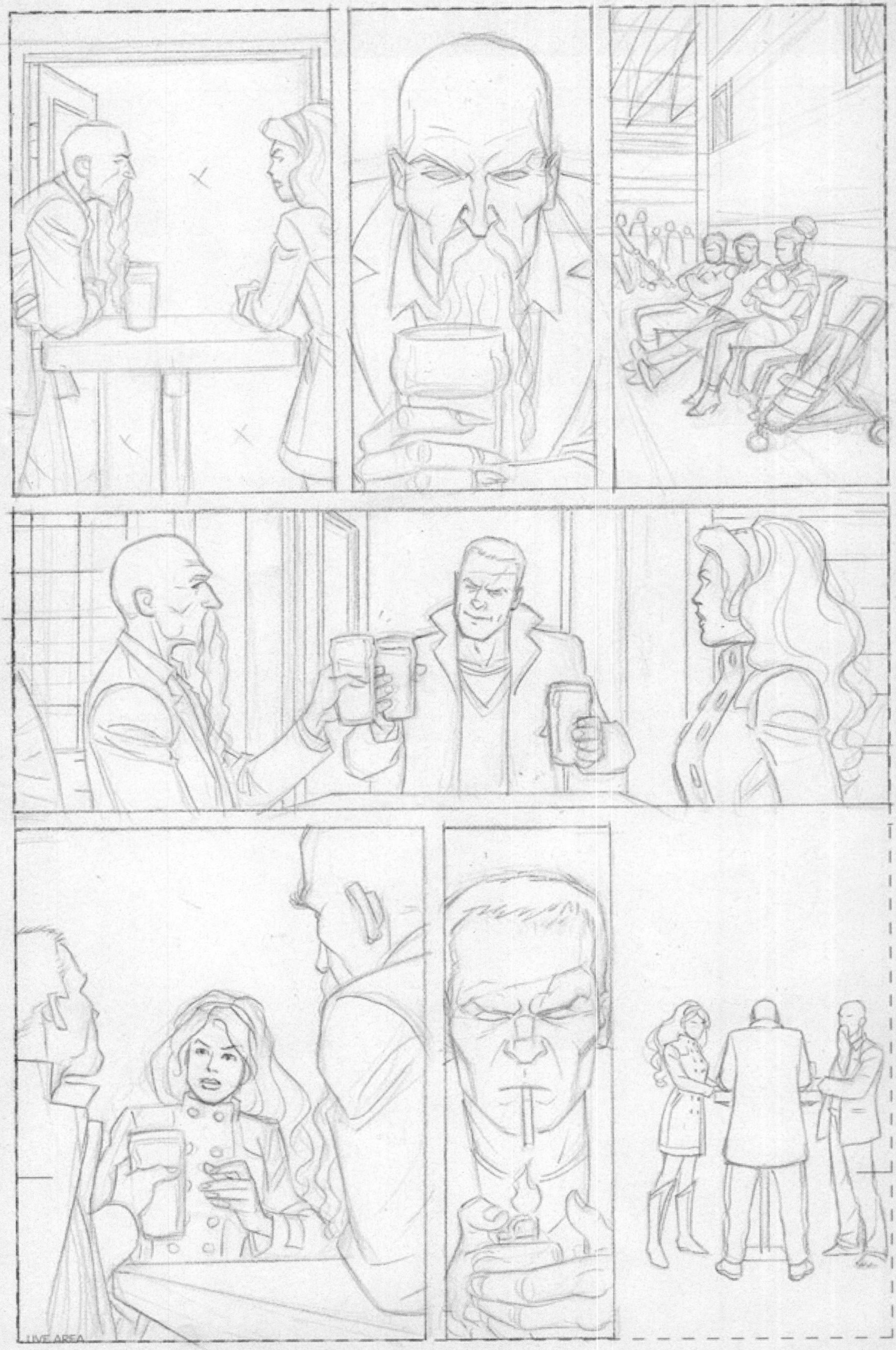
LIVE AREA

WONDER WOMAN 23 PLOT

We pick up right where we left off...

PAGE 1
Hyena man taunts WW, WW throws lasso, which main Hyena man dodges, but WW was aiming for a giant piece of rubble.

PAGE 2
WW swings lasso and takes out all nearby Hyena men. First Born laughs. "My family is bigger than yours."

PAGE 3
Reveal hordes of Hyena men around FB, moving towards group.

PAGE 4
War walks away from the group, mumbling to himself. He really seems like a doddering old man here. War knocks over either a wall or a column-- something that can create a lot of dust-- which it does. Dust fills the air, obscuring everything. FB laughs at War and his dust. "You can't hide from me, old man."

PAGE 5
Splash page. "Who's hiding?" Behind War is an army of warriors from all human history. Cavemen with clubs, Spartans, Goths, Romans, Crusaders, Redcoats, Nazis, WWII Marines, Viet Cong, etc.-- along with all their weaponry. It's epic.

PAGE 6
Hyena men and soldiers fight, as WW and War bond. I mean, he's going to have to tell her that he's proud of what she became, right? 4 panels. Last panel transition: Orion protects Hera and Zola (who grabs Hera's hand) from Hyena men.

PAGE 7
Hera and Zola bond, as they both try to protect each other. Zola pulls Hera in one direction, while Hera pulls in the other. Hera: "What do you think you're doing?" Zola: "Protecting you!" Hera: "No, I'M protecting YOU." They move past War's army towards abbey exit. Zola confides to Hera "Something tells me we're gonna be OK" – referring to Zeke, who is asleep.

PAGES 8-9
The Firstborn/Orion showdown. This has to be extremely brutal, with loads of dirty wrestling moves; eye gouges, bake rakes, low blows-- a real slobberknocker. Unlike last time, the First Born triumphs. Orion is powered by anger, War is powered by hate. Battle takes out back of church. Hate wins. FB crawls out of rubble.
Winded, he stands over Orion... as WW's cuffs hit the ground.

PAGE 10

FB swats soldiers away and makes his way towards War & WW. (What really has FB's attention is War; by killing him, he will take his throne. Our crew don't know this. It seems he's coming for WW.) War questions WW's strategy in fighting the First Born; brute strength vs. brute strength. WW assures him she knows what she's doing. "That doesn't make it smart," War counters. (Perhaps he'll also point out that WW is revealing to the world just how powerful she is. She'll counter that with, "Perhaps it needs to."

PAGES 11-13

The two-fisted meat-beating battle between WW & the FB. Go nuts. The thing is, everything she does, FB can take; it's almost as if he's conditioned to pain. One thing that does happen is WW begins to tire... and that's when FB strikes back. She's just an impediment to him-- War is the prize he wants. He makes quick work of WW. Before he can kill her, FB gets blasted with some machine gun fire (or something). It's War, holding the gun.

PAGE 14

FB threatens War. (War's army defends him-- if you can fit it in.) What's important is for Hera and Zola to rush to WW's aid. WW is beating herself up over her strategy, but there's no time for that! Get the cuffs on her.

PAGE 15
War puts up a good fight, but FB is just too much. He tells War he's going to kill him, fulfill the prophecy, take his throne, and then kill all the others. FB grabs War, and is going to kill him-- he'll get War's thrown, and take down Olympus from within. War sure looks done for... WW and War eye contact?... Fb is gloating... We need to see an energy flash from the cuffs...

PAGE 16
Let's go crazy... War pukes blood on FB's face. FB angrily whispers, "No..." Pull back. We see WW has driven a pike (or her sword) through War's back and into the FB. War hangs, dead. FB breaks the spear off, as WW catches War's body. (Or WW pulls the sword out.)

PAGES 17-18
WW cradles War... tender moment. He's proud of her, but also very sorry for the burden he's given her. He also tells her that he wasn't the first, and she won't be the last. While this is going on, an angry FB falls to his knees. WW is crying. He's like a dog that won't quit fighting, he's swinging at the air, desperately trying to get at War and kill him. Now, he can either run out of energy and pass out, or maybe Hera and Zola whack him, and knock him out. It can go either way.

War dies.

Just so you know, I think she would kill him dead while he's in FB's clutches, thereby ending the threat. And the melodrama.

(Also, should we do a dorky Highlander shtick and have some sort of energy plasma swirl around WW to show she's the God of War now? My gut says no, but it's been wrong before...)

PAGES 19-20

As WW cradles a dead War, a hand appears on her shoulder; it's Hades, & he's there for his brother. Might as well have his boat there too, maybe sailing on mist and haze. WW picks up War and takes him to the boat-- or War "floats" to the boat, if you'd like Hades & WW to hold hands. We should have a Hera moment too, as War was her son. Something along the lines of "He'll know something he's never known before... peace." The FB is passed along the way, and WW asks about him. Hades tells her he's not dead, but if she'd like to finish him... "No. There's been enough killing today."

WW and Hades sail away (with our crew too?) and we see that they were being watched by Apollo. He walks over to the FB, and smiles. The boat sails away. (I figure this will be accompanied by WW & Hades V/O, and he calls her the God of War.)

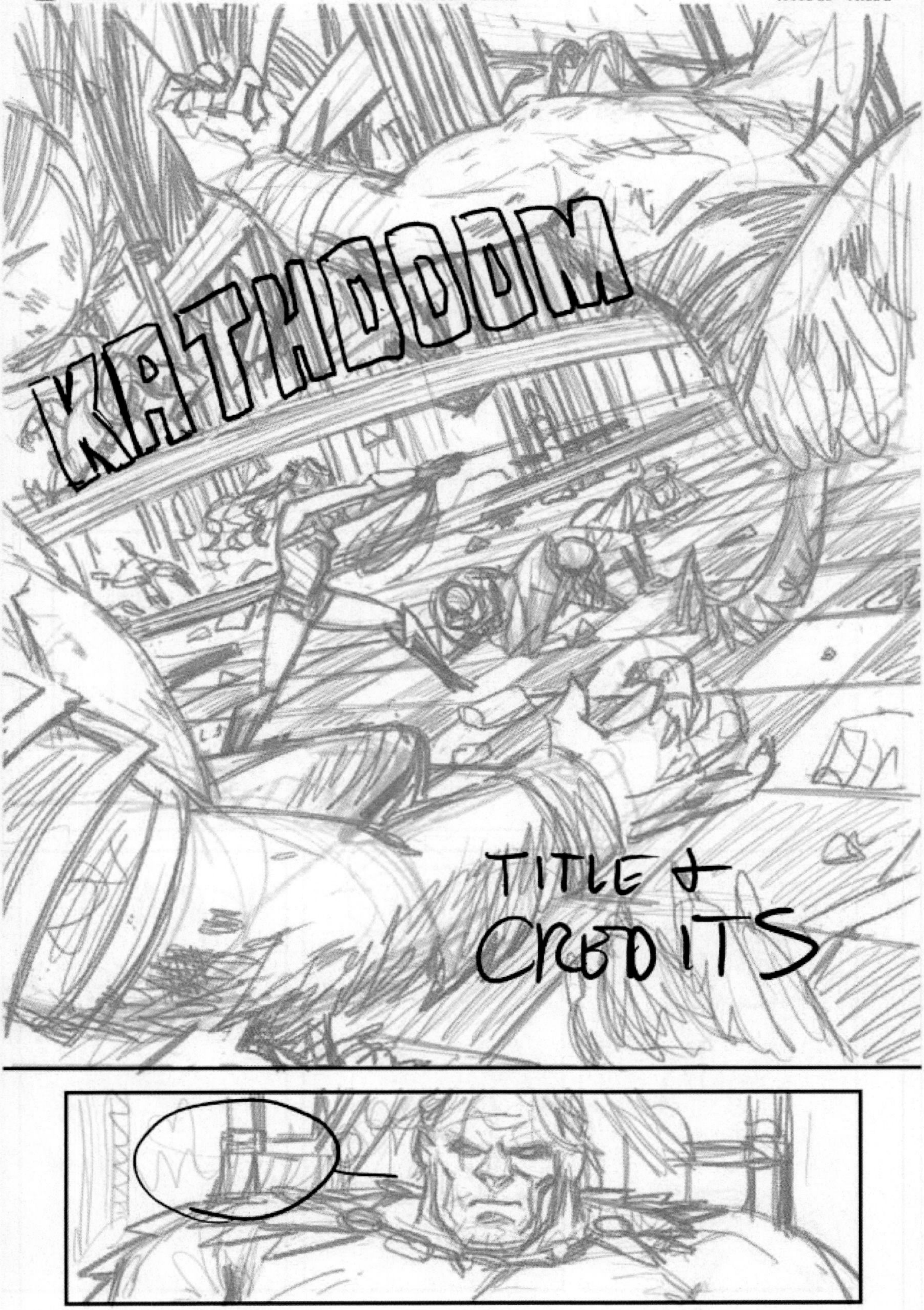
KATHOOOM
TITLE &
CREDITS

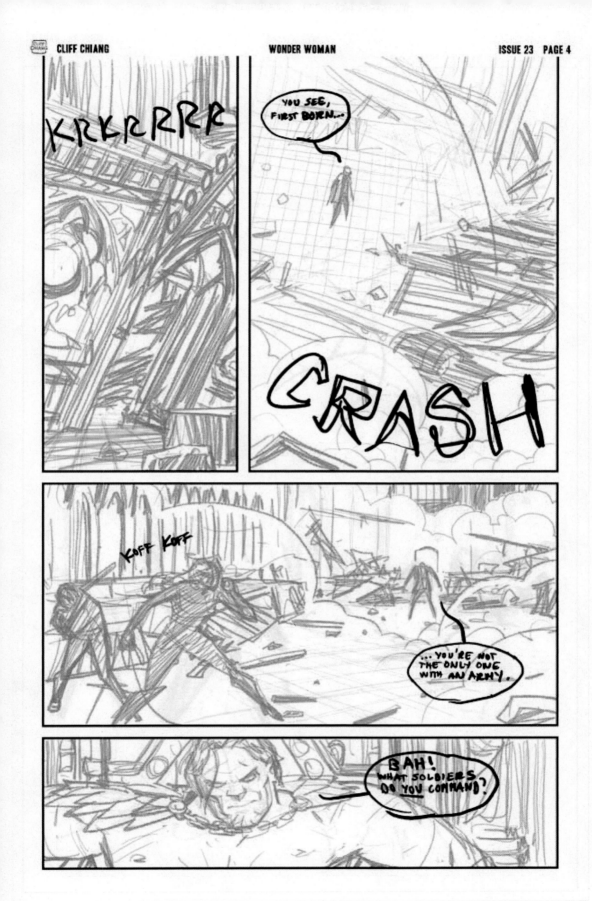

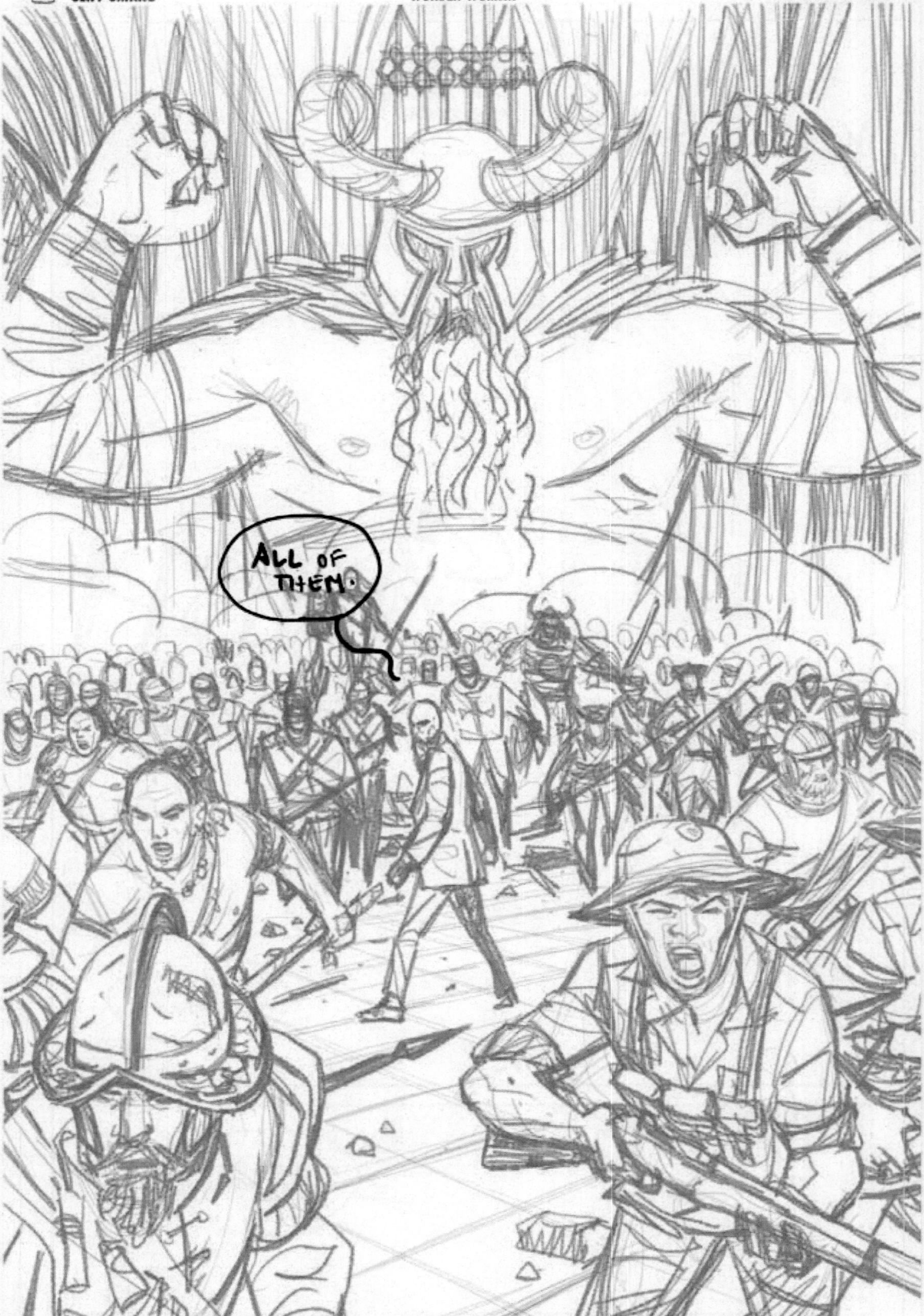
ALL OF THEM.

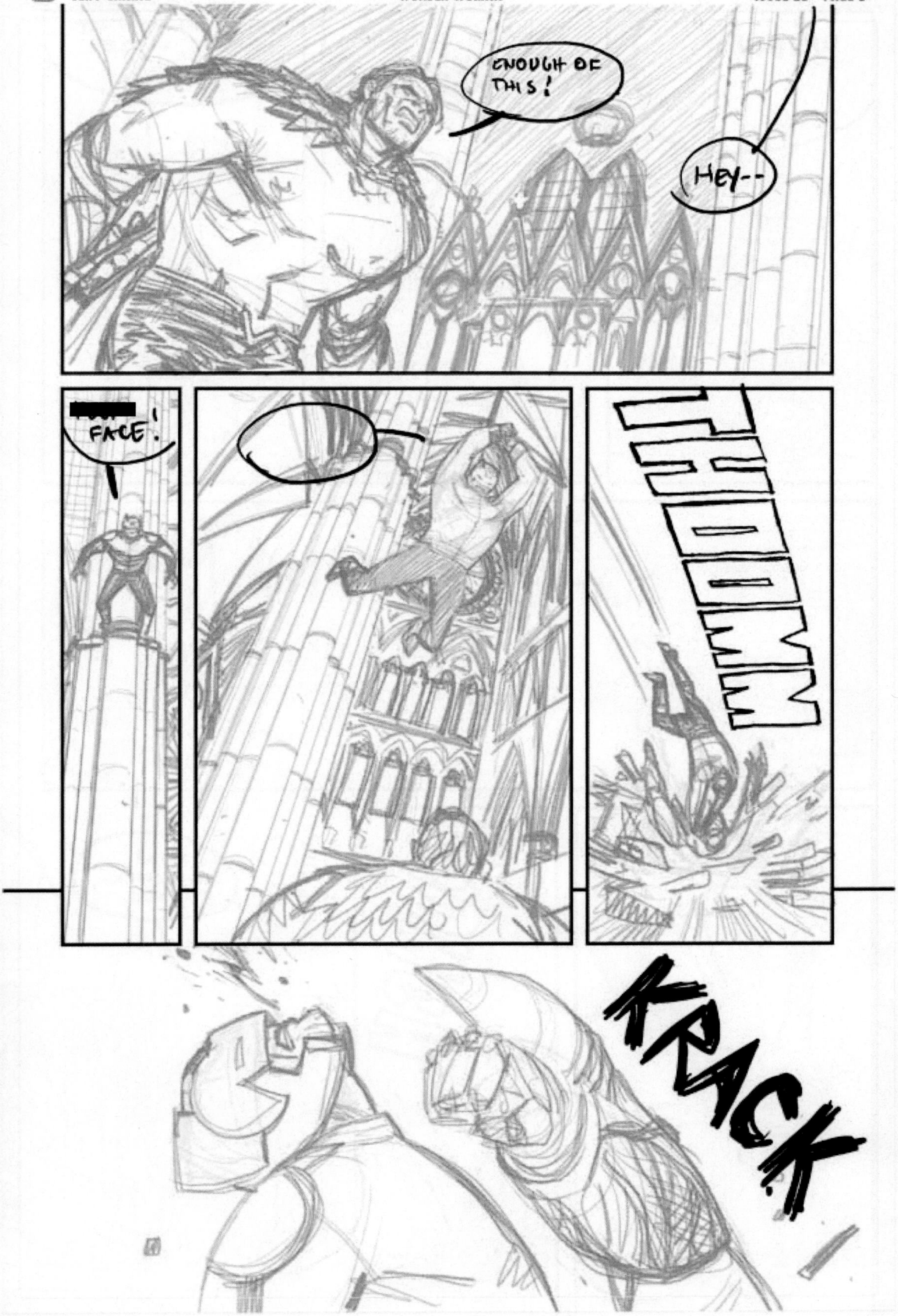
ENOUGH OF THIS!
Hey--
[redacted] FACE!
THOOMM
KRACK

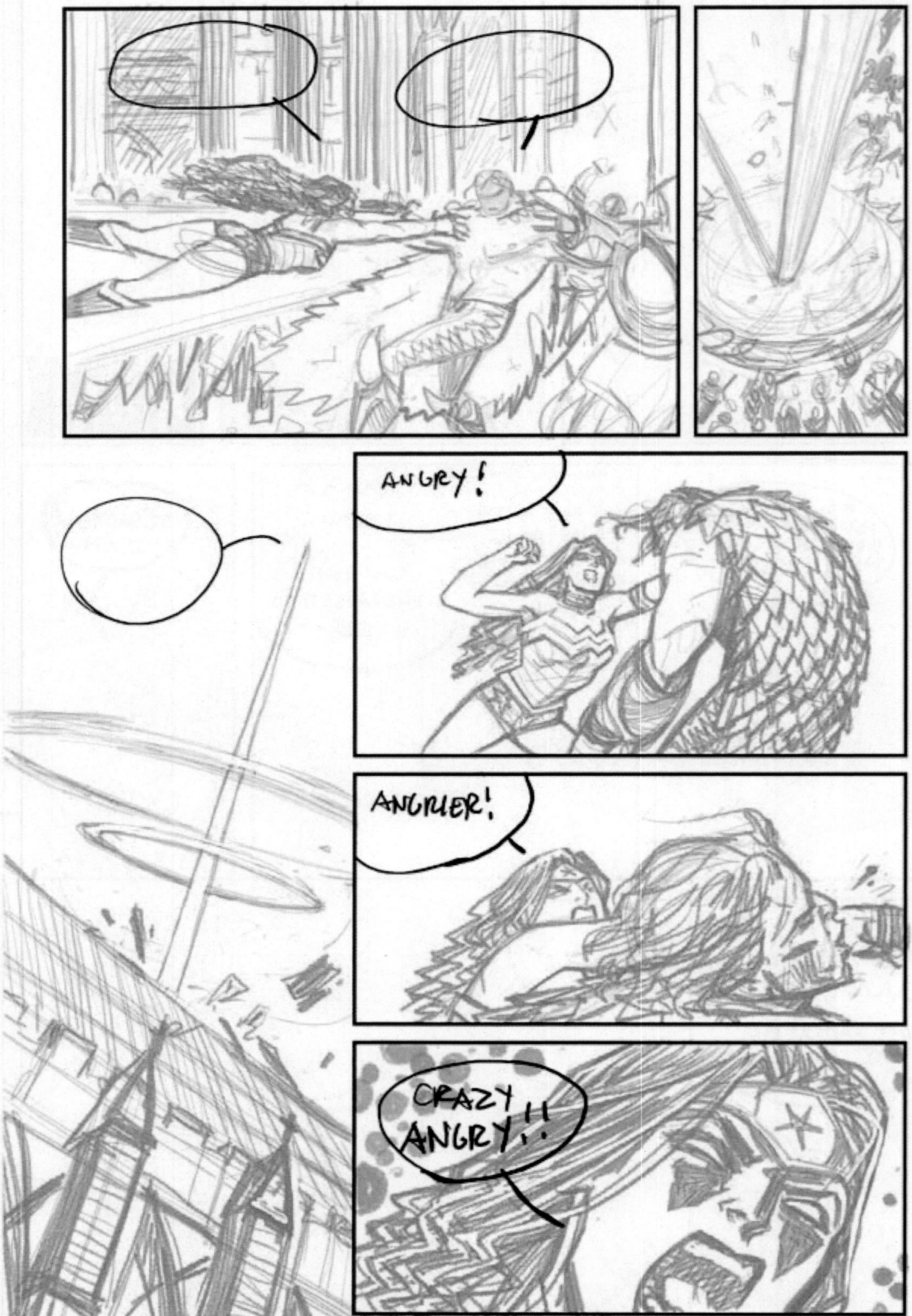
ANGRY!
ANGRIER!
CRAZY ANGRY!!!

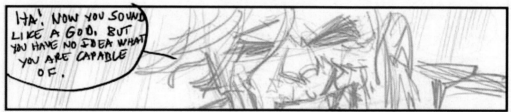

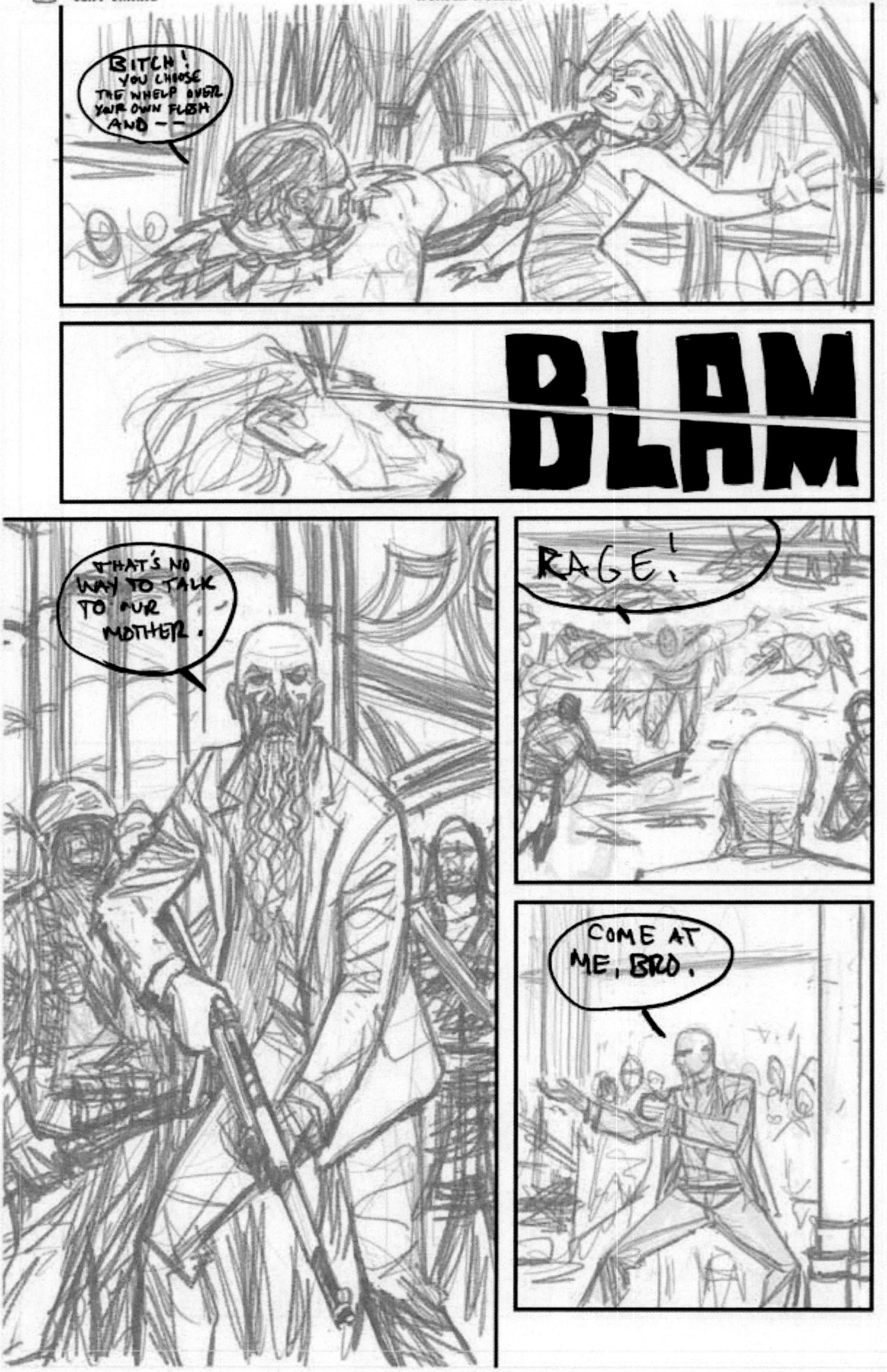
BITCH! YOU CHOOSE THE WHELP OVER YOUR OWN FLESH AND--
BLAM
THAT'S NO WAY TO TALK TO OUR MOTHER.
RAGE!
COME AT ME, BRO.

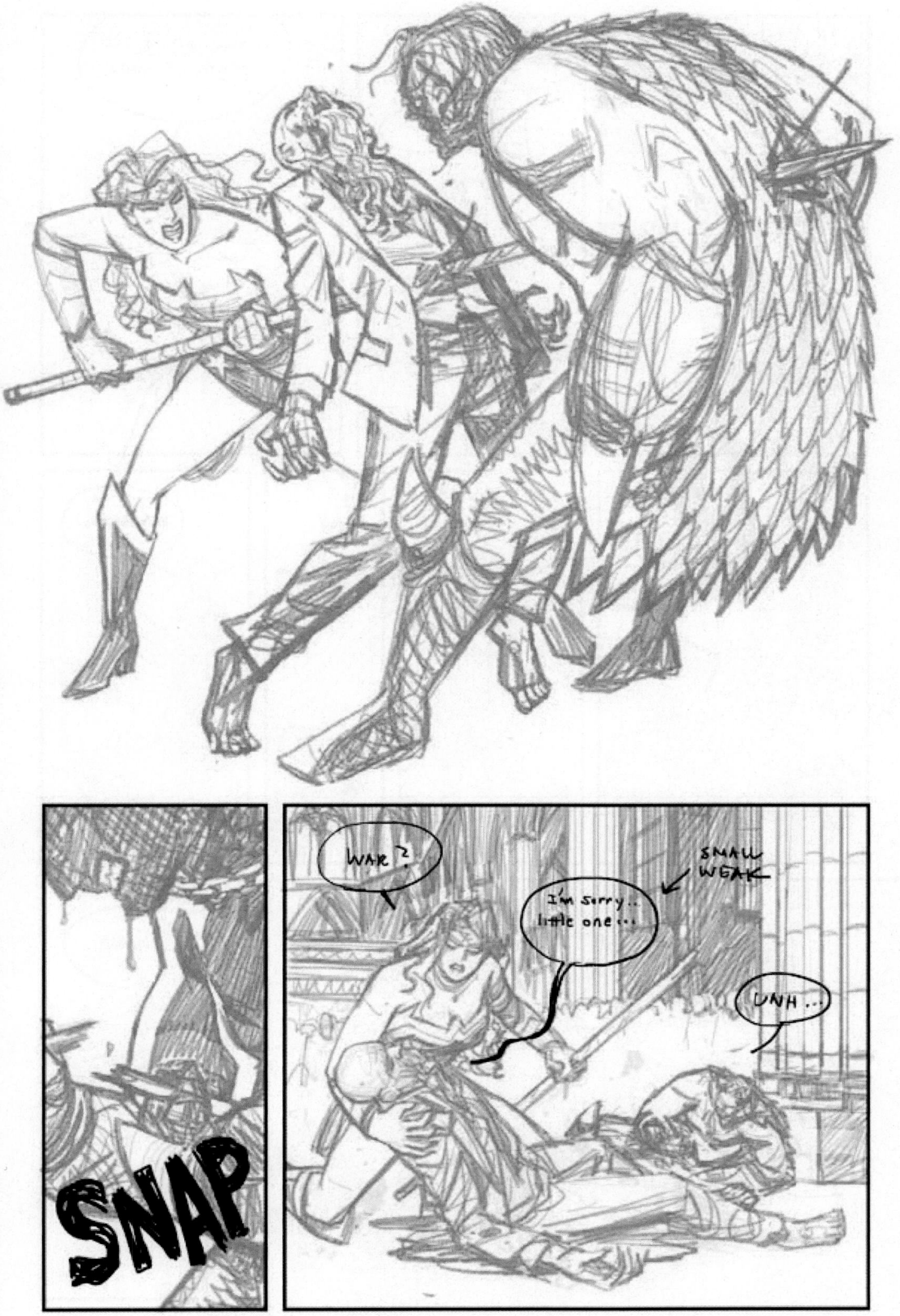
SNAP
WAR?
I'm sorry... little one...
SMALL WEAK
UNH...

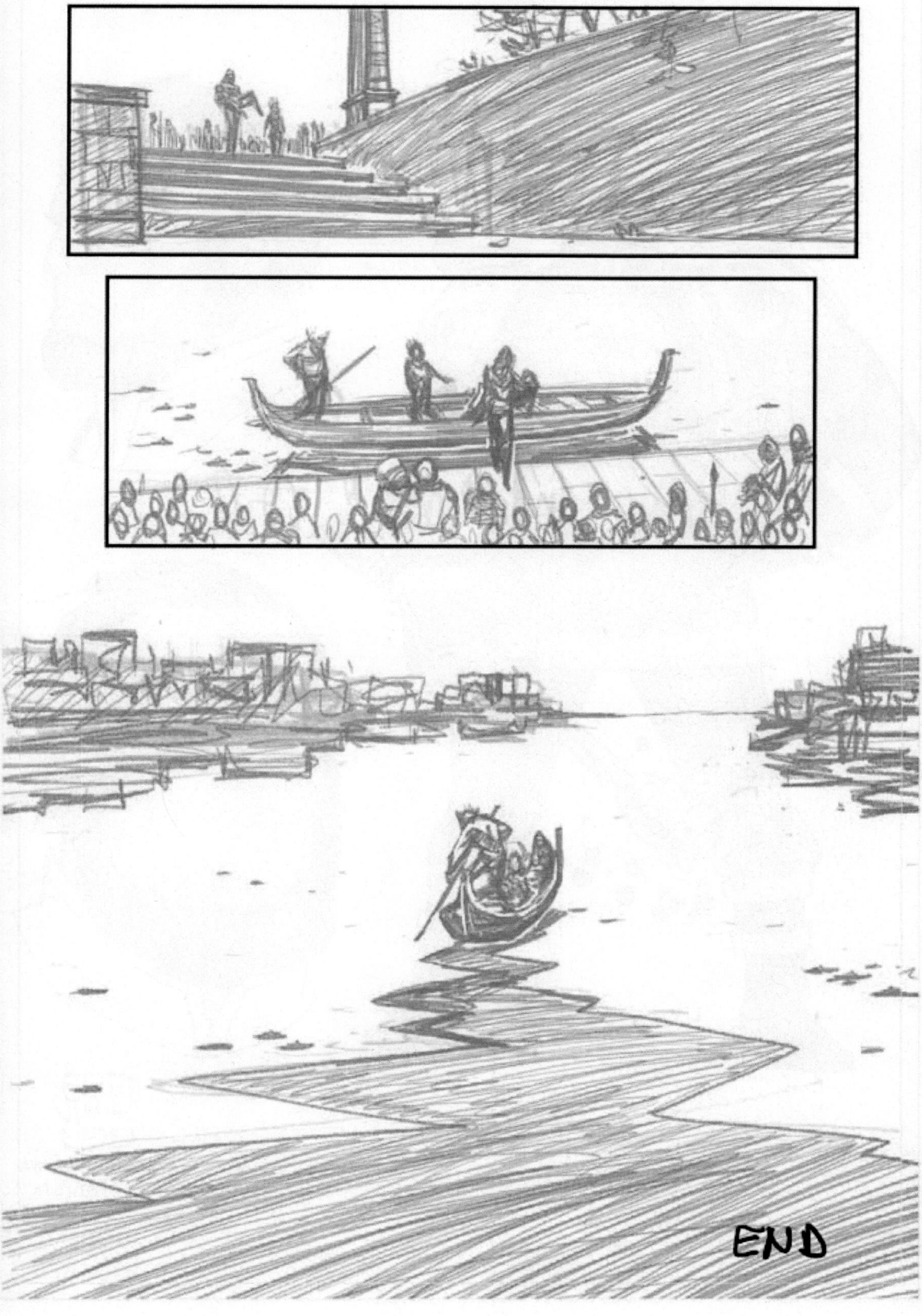
END

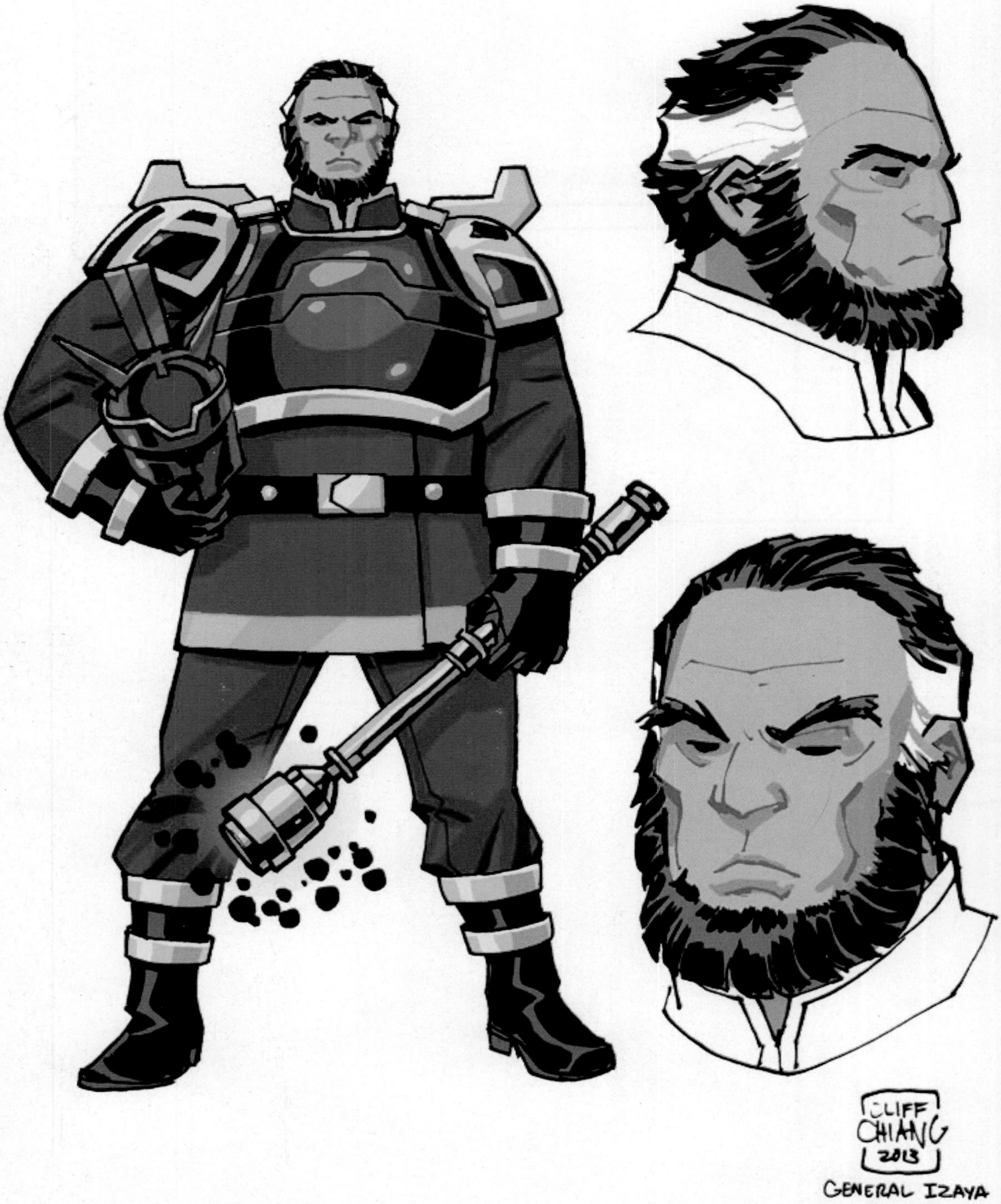
CLIFF
CHIANG
2013
GENERAL IZAYA
"HIGHFATHER"